Picked-By-You Guides®

Top Rated Outdoor Series

Top Rated™
Bird Hunting

Upland, Turkey and Waterfowl
in North America

by Maurizio Valerio

PICKED-BY-YOU GUIDES®

Top Rated Outdoor Series

Copies of this book can be ordered from:

Picked-By-You

PO Box 718

Baker City, OR 97814

Phone: (800) 279-0479 • Fax: (541) 523-5028

www.topguides.com • e-mail: maurice@topguides.com

Artwork by Steamroller Studios, Cover Art by Fifth Street Design
Maps by Map Art, Cartesia Software
Printed in Korea

Publisher's Cataloging-in-Publication
(Provided by Quality Books, Inc.)

Valerio, Maurice.
    Top rated bird hunting : upland, turkey and waterfowl in North America / by Maurizio Valerio. -- 1st ed.
    p. cm. -- (Top rated outdoor series)
    Includes indexes.
    Preassigned LCCN: 98-67992
    ISBN: 1-889807-12-5

    1. Fowling--North America--Directories.   2. Hunting guides --North America--Directories.   3. Hunting lodges--North America--Directories.   I. Title.

SK12. V35 1999   799.2'4'0257
                                        QBI98-1374

To Allison, Marco and Nini

About the Author

Maurizio (Maurice) Valerio received a Doctoral degree Summa cum Laude in Natural Science, majoring in Animal Behaviour, from the University of Parma (Italy) in 1981, and a Master of Arts degree in Zoology from the University of California, Berkeley in 1984.

He is a rancher, a writer and a devoted outdoorsman who decided to live with the wild animals that he cherishes so much in the Wallowa Mountains of Northeast Oregon. He has traveled extensively in the Old and New World, for more than 25 years. He is dedicated to preserving everyone's individual right of a respectful, knowledgeable and diversified use of our Outdoor Resources.

Table of Contents

Acknowledgments

It is customary in this section to give credit to those who have contributed to the realization of the end product. The Picked-By-You Guides® started three years ago as a little personal crusade and has evolved into a totally challenging, stimulating and rewarding full time commitment.

My deep thanks must go first to all the Captains, Ranchers, Guides, Lodges and Outfitters who decided to trust our honesty and integrity. They have taken a leap of faith in sharing their lists of clients with us and for this we are truly honored and thankful.

They have constantly encouraged our idea. Captains have taught us the difference between skinny fishing and skinny dipping, while River Guides have patiently help us to identify rafters , purlins , catarafts and J-rig rafts. They were also ready to give us a badly needed push forward every time this very time-consuming idea came to a stall. We have come to know many of them through pleasant phone chats, e-mails, faxes and letters. They now sound like old friends on the phone and we are certain we all share a deep respect for the mountains, the deserts and the waters of this great country of ours.

The Picked-By-You Team (both in the office and abroad), with months of hard work, skills, ingenuity, good sense of humor and pride, have then transformed a simple good idea into something a bit more tangible and much more exciting. They all have put their hearts in the concept and their hands and feet in the dirt. Some with a full-time schedule, some with a part-time collaboration, all of them bring their unique and invaluable style and contribution.

My true thanks to Brent Beck, Lindsay Benson, Bob Erdmann, Robert Evans, Cheryl Fisher, Brian Florence, Sally Georgeson, Grace Martin, Kevin McNamara, Jerry Meek, Allison C. Mickens, Tom Novak, Shelby Sherrod, Dyanne Van Swoll, Giuseppe Verdi and Mr. Peet's Coffee and Tea.

Last, but not least, my sincere, profound, and loving gratitude to my wife Allison. Her patient support, her understanding, her help and her skills have been the fuel which started and stoked this fire. Her laughter has been the wind to fan it.

To you Allie, with a toast to the next project…just kidding!

Maurizio (Maurice) Valerio

Preface

The value of information depends on its usefulness. Simply put, whatever allows you to make informed choices will be to your advantage. To that end, Picked-By-You Guides® aims to take the guesswork out of selecting services for outdoor activities. Did you get what you paid for? From Picked-By-You Guides®' point of view, the most reliable indicator is customer satisfaction.

The information in this book is as reliable as those who chose to participate. In the process of selecting the top professionals, Picked-By-You Guides® contacted all licensed guides, outfitters and businesses which provide services for outdoor activities. They sought to include everyone but not all who were contacted agreed to participate according to the rules. Thus, the omission of a guide, outfitter or service does not automatically mean they didn't qualify based on customer dissatisfaction.

The market abounds with guidebooks by 'experts' who rate a wide range of services based on their personal preferences. The value of the Picked-By-You concept is that businesses earn a place in these books only when they receive favorable ratings from a majority of clients. If ninety percent of the customers agree that their purchase of services met or exceeded their expectations, then it's realistic to assume that you will also be satisfied when you purchase services from the outdoor professionals and businesses included in this book.

It's a fact of life; not everyone is satisfied all of the time or by the same thing. Individual experiences are highly subjective and are quite often based on expectations. One person's favorable response to a situation might provoke the opposite reaction in another. A novice might be open to any experience without any preconceived notions while a veteran will be disappointed when anything less than great expectations aren't met.

If you select any of the businesses in this book, chances are excellent that you will know what you are buying. A diversity of clients endorsed them because they believed the services they received met or exceeded their expectations. Picked-By-You Guides® regards that information more valuable than a single observer or expert's point of view.

The intent behind Picked-By-You Guides® is to protect the consumer from being misled or deceived. It is obvious that these clients were given accurate information which resulted in a positive experience and a top rating.

The number of questionnaire responses which included detailed and sometimes lengthy comments impressed upon us the degree to which people value their experiences. Many regard them as "once-in-a-lifetime" and "priceless," and they heaped generous praise on those whose services made it possible.

Picked-By-You Guides® has quantified the value of customer satisfaction and created a greater awareness of top-rated outdoor professionals. It remains up to you to choose and be the judge of your own experience. With the help of this book, you will have the advantage of being better informed when making that pick.

Robert Evans, *information specialist*

The Picked-By-You Guides® Idea

Mission Statement

The intent of this publication is to provide the outdoor enthusiast and his/her family with an objective and easy-to-read reference source that would list only those businesses and outdoor professionals who have **agreed to be rated** and have been overwhelmingly endorsed by their past clients.

There are many great outdoor professionals (Guides, Captains, Ranches, Lodges, Outfitters) who deserve full recognition for putting their experience, knowledge, long hours, and big heart, into this difficult job. With this book we want to reward those deserving professionals while providing an invaluable tool to the general public.

Picked-By-You Guides® are the only consumer guides to outdoor activities.

In this respect it would be useful to share the philosophy of our Company succinctly illustrated by our Mission Statement:

> "To encourage and promote the highest professional and ethical standards among those individuals, Companies, Groups or Organizations who provide services to the Outdoor Community.

To communicate and share the findings and values of our research and surveys to the public and other key groups.

To preserve everyone's individual right of a respectful, knowledgeable and diversified use of our Outdoor Resources".

Our business niche is well defined and our job is simply to listen carefully.

THEY 'the experts' Vs. WE 'the People'

Picked-By-You books were researched and compiled by **asking people such as yourself**, who rafted, fished, hunted or rode a horse on a pack trip with a particular outdoor professional or business, to rate their services, knowledge, skills and performance.

Only the ones who received A- to A+ scores from their clients are found listed in these pages.

The market is flooded with various publications written by 'experts' claiming to be the ultimate source of information for your vacation. We read books with titles such as " The Greatest River Guides", "The Complete Guide to the Greatest Fishing Lodges" etc.

We do not claim to be experts in any given field, but we rather pass to history as good....listeners. In the preparation of the Questionnaires we listened first to the outdoor professionals' point of view and then to the comments and opinions of thousands of outdoor enthusiasts. We then organized the findings of our research and surveys in this and other publications of this series.

Thus we will not attempt to tell how to fish, how to paddle or what to bring on your trip. We are leaving this to the outdoor professionals featured in this book, for they have proven to be outstanding in providing much valuable information before, during and after your trip.

True [paid] advertising: an oxymoron

Chili with beans is considered a redundant statement for the overwhelming majority of cooks but it is an insulting oxymoron for any native Texan.

In the same way while 'true paid advertising' is a correct statement for some, it is a clear contradiction in terms for us and certainly many of you. A classic oxymoron.

This is why we do not accept commissions, donations, invitations, or, as many publishers cleverly express it, "...extra fees to help defray the cost of publication". Many articles are written every month in numerous specialized magazines in which the authors tour the country from lodge to lodge and camp to camp sponsored, invited, or otherwise compensated in many different shapes or forms.

It is indeed a form of direct advertising and, although this type of writing usually conveys a good amount of general information, in most cases it lacks the impartiality so valuable when it comes time to make the final selection for your vacation or outdoor adventure.

Without belittling the invaluable job of the professional writers and their integrity, we decided to approach the task of **researching information and sharing it with the public** with a different angle and from an opposite direction.

Money? .. No thanks!

We are firmly **committed to preserve the impartiality** and the novelty of the Picked-By-You idea.

For this reason we want to reassure the reader that the outdoor professionals and businesses featured in this book have not paid (nor will they pay), any remuneration to Picked-by-You Guides ® or the author in the form of money, invitations or any other considerations.

They have earned a valued page in this book solely as the result of *their hard work and dedication to their clients.*

"A spot in this book cannot be purchased: it must be earned"

Size of a business in not a function of its performance

Since the embryonic stage of the Picked-By-You idea, during the compilation of the first Picked-By-You book, we faced a puzzling dilemma.

Should we establish a minimum number of clients under which a business or outdoor professional will not be allowed to participate in our evaluating process?

This would be a 'safe' decision when it comes the time to elaborate the responses of the questionnaires. But we quickly learned that many outdoor professionals limit, by choice, the total number of clients and, by philosophy of life, contain and control the size of their business. They do not want to grow too big and sacrifice the personal touches or the freshness of their services. In their words "we don't want to take the chance to get burned out by people." They do not consider their activity just a job, but rather a way of living.

"WHY, NO MAM, WE NEVER HAVE HAD ANY OF THOSE SASQUATCH SIGHTINGS IN THESE PARTS."

But if this approach greatly limits the number of clients accepted every year we must say that these outdoor professionals are the ones who often receive outstanding ratings and truly touching comments from their past clients.

Some businesses have provided us with a list of clients of 40,000, some with 25 . In this book **you will find both the large and the small.**

From a statistical point, it is obvious that a fly fishing guide who submitted a list of 32 clients, by virtue of the sample size of the individuals surveyed, will implicitly have a lower level of accuracy if compared to a business for which we surveyed 300 guests. (Please refer to the Rating and Data

Elaboration Sections for details on how we established the rules for qualification and thus operated our selection).

We do not believe that the size of business is a function of its good performance and we feel strongly that those dedicated professionals who choose to remain small deserve an equal chance to be included.

We tip our hats

We want to recognize all the Guides, Captains, Ranches, Lodges and Outfitters who have participated in our endeavor, whether they qualified or not. The fact alone that they accepted to be rated by their past clients is a clear indication of how much they care, and how willing they are to make changes.

We also want to credit all those outdoor enthusiasts who have taken the time to complete the questionnaires and share their memories and impressions with us and thus with you. Some of the comments sent to us were hilarious, some were truly touching.

We were immensely pleased by the reaction of the outdoor community at large. The idea of "Picked-by-You Guides®" was supported from the beginning by serious professionals and outdoor enthusiasts alike. We listened to their suggestions, their comments, their criticisms and we are now happy to share this information with you.

Questionnaires

"Our books will be only as good as the questions we ask."

We posted this phrase in the office as a reminder of the importance of the 'tool' of this trade. The questions.

Specific Questionnaires were tailored to each one of the different activities surveyed for this series of books. While a few of the general questions remained the same throughout, many were specific to particular activities. The final objective of the questionnaire was to probe the many different facets of that diversified field known as the outdoors.

The first important factor we had to consider in the preparation of the Questionnaires was the total number of questions to be asked. Research shows an *inversely proportionate relation* between the total number of questions and the percentage of the response: the higher the number of questions, the lower the level of response. Thus we had to balance an acceptable return rate with a meaningful significance. We settled for a compromise and we decided to keep 20 as the maximum number.

The first and the final versions of the Questionnaires on which we based our surveys turned out to be very different. We asked all the businesses and outdoor professionals we contacted for suggestions and criticisms. They helped us a great deal: we weighed their different points of view and we incorporated all their suggestions into the final versions.

We initially considered using a phone survey, but we quickly agreed with the businesses and outdoor professional that we all are already bothered by too many solicitation calls when we are trying to have a quiet dinner at home. We do not want you to add Picked-By-You to the list of companies that you do not want to talk to, nor we want you to add our 800 number to your caller ID black list.

In using the mail we knew that we were going to have a slightly lower percentage of questionnaires answered, but this method is, in our opinion, a more respectful one.

We also encouraged the public to participate in the designing of the questionnaire by posting on our Web at www.topguides.com the opportunity to submit a question and …."Win a book". Many sent their suggestions and , if they were chosen to be used in one of our questionnaires, they were given the book of their choice.

Please send us your question and/or your suggestions for our future surveys at:

PICKED-BY-YOU Guides®, P.O. Box 718, Baker City, OR 97814

Rating (there is more than one way to skin the cat)

We considered many different ways to score the questionnaires, keeping in mind at all times our task:

translate an opinion into a numerical value

Some of the approaches considered were simple *averages* [arithmetical means], others were sophisticated statistical tests. In the end we opted for simplicity, sacrificing to the God of statistical significance. WARNING: if $p \leq 0.001$ has any meaning in your life stop reading right here: you will be disappointed with the rest.

For the rest of us, we also made extensive use in our computation of the *median*, a statistic of location, which divides the frequency distribution of a set of data into two halves. A quick example, with our imaginary Happy Goose Outfitter, will illustrate how in many instances the *median* value, being the center observation, helps describing the distribution, which is the truly weak point of the *average*:

Average salary at Happy Goose Outfitters $ 21,571

Median salary at Happy Goose Outfitters $ 11,000

5,000	10,000	10,000	11,000	12,000	15,000	98,000
Wrangler	Guide	Guide	Senior Guide	Asst.Cook	Cook	Boss

Do not ask the boss : "What's the average salary?"

These are the values assigned to **Questions 1-15**:

5.00 points	OUTSTANDING
4.75 points	EXCELLENT
4.25 points	GOOD
3.50 points	ACCEPTABLE
3.00 points	POOR
0.00 points	UNACCEPTABLE

Question 16, relating to the weather conditions, was treated as bonus points to be added to the final score.

Good=0   Fair=1   Poor=2

The intention here was to reward the outdoor professional who had to work in adverse weather conditions.

Questions 17 - 18 = 5 points

Questions 19 - 20 = 10 points

The individual scores of each Questionnaire were expressed as a percentage to avoid the total score from being drastically affected by one question left unanswered or marked "not applicable." All the scores received for each individual outdoor professional and business were thus added and computed.

The 90 points were considered our cutoff point. Note how the outfitters must receive a combination of Excellent with only a few Good marks (or better) in order to qualify.

Only the Outfitters, Captains, Lodges, Guides who received an A- to A+ score did qualify and they are featured in this book.

We also decided not to report in the book pages the final scores with which the businesses and the outdoor professionals ultimately qualified. In a way we thought that this could be distractive.

In the end, we must admit, it was tough to leave out some outfitters who scored very close to the cutoff mark.

It would be presumptuous to think that our scoring system will please everybody, but we want to assure the reader that we tested different computations of the data. We feel the system that we have chosen respects the overall opinion of the guest/client and maintains a more than acceptable level of accuracy.

We know that .... "You can change without improving, but you cannot improve without changing."

The Power of Graphs (how to lie by telling the scientific truth)

The following examples illustrate the sensational (and unethical) way with which the 'scientific' computation of data can be distorted to suit one's needs or goals.

The *Herald* presents a feature article on the drastic increase of total tonnage of honey stolen by bears (mostly Poohs) in a given area during 1997.

Total tonnage of honey stolen by bears (Poohs)

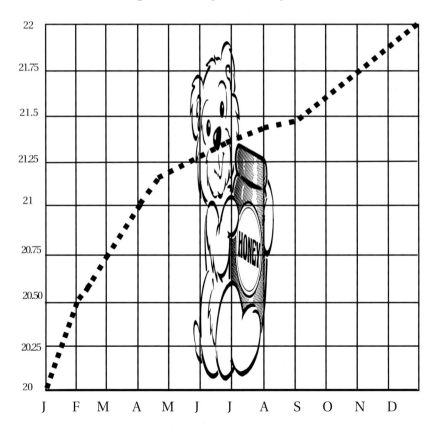

Total tonnage of honey stolen by bears (Poohs)

It is clear how a journalist, researcher or author must ultimately choose one type of graph. But the question here is whether or not he/she is trying to make "his/her point" by choosing one type versus the other, rather than simply communicate some findings.

Please note that the bears, in our example, are shameless, and remain such in both instances, for they truly love honey!

Graphs were not used in this book. We were just too worried we wouldn't use the correct ones.

The Book Making Process

Research

We **researched** the name and address of every business and outdoor professional **in the United States and** in all the **provinces of Canada** (see list in the Appendix). Some states do not require guides and outfitters or businesses providing outdoor services to be registered, and in these instances the information must be obtained from many different sources [Outfitter's Associations, Marine Fisheries, Dept. of Tourism, Dept. Environmental Conservation, Dept. of Natural Resources, Dept. of Fish and Game, US Coast Guard, Chamber of Commerce, etc.].

In the end the database on which we based this series of Picked-By-You Guides® amounted to more than 23,000 names of Outfitters, Guides, Ranches, Captains etc. Our research continues and this number is increasing every day. The Appendix in the back of this book is only a partial list and refers specifically to Top Rated Bird Hunting.

Participation

We **invited** businesses and outdoor professionals, with a letter and a brochure explaining the Picked-By-You concept, to join our endeavor by simply sending us a **complete** **list of their clients** of the past two years. With the "Confidentiality Statement" we reassured them that the list was going to be kept **absolutely confidential** and to be *used one time only* for the specific purpose of evaluating their operation. Then it would be destroyed.

We truly oppose this "black market" of names so abused by the mail marketing business. If you are ever contacted by Picked-By-You you may rest assured that your name, referred to us by your outdoor professional, will never be sold, traded or otherwise used a second time by us for marketing purposes.

Questionnaires

We then **sent a questionnaire** to **every single client on each** list (to a maximum of 300 randomly picked for those who submitted large lists with priority given to overnight or multiple day trips), asking

them to rate the **services**, the **knowledge** and **performance** of the business or outdoor professional by completing our comprehensive questionnaire (see pages 142-147). The businesses and outdoor professionals found in these pages may or may not be the ones who invest large sums of money to advertise in magazines, or to participate at the annual conventions of different clubs and foundations. However, they are clearly the ones, according to our survey, that put customer satisfaction and true dedication to their clients first and foremost.

Data Elaboration

A **numerical value was assigned to each question**. All the **scores were computed**. Both the **average** and the **median** were calculated and considered for eligibility. Please note that the total score was computed as a percentile value.

This allows some flexibility where one question was left unanswered or was answered with a N/A. Furthermore, we decided not to consider the high and the low score to ensure a more evenly distributed representation and to reduce the influence which an extreme judgement could have either way (especially with the small sample sizes).

We also set a **minimum number of questionnaires** which needed to be answered to allow a business or an outdoor professional to qualify. Such number was set as a function of the total number of clients in the list: the smaller the list of clients, the higher was the percentage of responses needed for qualification.

In some cases the outfitter's average score came within 1 points of the A-cutoff mark. In these instances, we considered both the median and the average were considered as well as the guests' comments and the total number of times that this particular business was recommended by the clients by answering with a 'yes' question 19 and 20.

Sharing the results

Picked-By-You will share the results of this survey with the businesses and the outdoor professionals. This will be done at no cost to them whether or not they qualified for publication. All questionnaires received will, in fact, be returned along with a summary result to the business, keeping the confidentiality of the client's name when this was requested. This will prove an invaluable tool to help improving those areas that have received some criticisms.

The intention of this series of books is to research the opinions and the comments of outdoor enthusiasts, and to share the results of our research with the public and other key groups.

One outfitter wrote us about our Picked-by-You Guides® series, "I feel your idea is an exciting and unique concept. Hopefully our past clientele will rate us with enough points to 'earn' a spot in your publication. If not, could we please get a copy of our points/questionnaires to see where we need to improve. Sincerely…"

This outfitter failed to qualify by just a few points, but such willingness to improve leaves us no doubt that his/her name will be one of those featured in our second edition. In the end it was not easy to exclude some of them from publication, but we are certain that, with the feedback provided by this survey, they will be able to improve those areas that need extra attention.

We made a real effort to keep a position of absolute impartiality in this process and, in this respect, we would like to repeat that the outfitters have not paid, nor they will pay, one single penny to Picked-By-You Guides® or the Author to be included in this book.

The research continues.

Icon Legend
General Services and Accommodations

Family

Kids

Senior Citizen

Full Board

Lodge

Hotel/Motel

Cabin

Trailer

Wall Tent Camp

Hot Springs/Spas

Archeological Sites

Swimming Pool

Icon Legend
General Services and Accommodations

Handicap

Women Only Camps/Dates

Natural /Gourmet Meals

Dog Kennels

Tennis

Unguided Activities

Guided Activities

Taxidermy Preparation

Overnight Trips

Day Trips

Bird Cleaning Service

Icon Legend
Locations

Lake

River

Dry Field

Stream/Creek

Wetlands

Season(s) of Operation

Fall

Year-round

Summer

Winter

Spring

Icon Legend
Activities

River Hunts for
Upland or Waterfowl

Clay Shooting (Trap,
Skeet, Sporting Clay)

Wildlife Observation

Horseback Riding Hunts

Wagon Hunts

Tree Stand for Hunting/
Photography

Blinds for Waterfowl
and Turkey Hunting

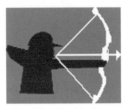

Bow Hunting/Archery

Fly Fishing

Upland Bird Hunting

Big Game Hunting

Pointers Provided

Retrievers Provided

Icon Legend
Birds

Sage Grouse

Pheasant

Ruffed Grouse

Prairie Chicken(s)

Sharptail Grouse

Hungarian (Gray) Partridge

Chukar

Northern Bobwhite

California Quail

Scaled (Blue) Quail

Icon Legend
Birds

Turkey(s) [Eastern, Florida, Gould's, Merriam's, Occellated, Rio Grande]

Snipe

Canada Goose (and all Geese species)

Woodcock

Snow Goose

Sea Ducks and Bay Ducks (all species)

Mallard and (all Dabbling Ducks)

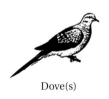

Sandhill Crane

Dove(s)

Icon Legend
Transportation

Amphibious Vehicle

Quad / ATV

House Boat

Airplane On Floaters

Jon Boat

Canoe

Raft

Horseback

Jet Boat

Motor Boat

Hovercraft

Jeep

Snowmobile

Bird Hunting
Outfitters, Guides, Preserves and Lodges

Alaska

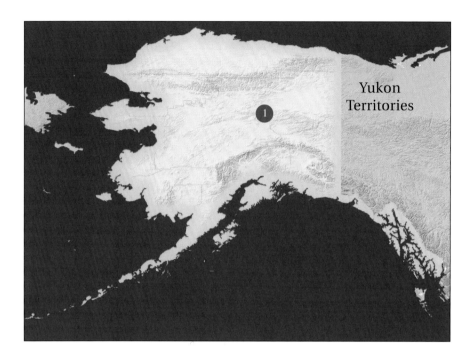

Outdoor Professionals

1 Eagles' Ridge Ranch

License and Report Requirements

• State requires licensing of Outdoor Professionals.

• State requires a "Hunt Record" for big game.

• State to implement a "logbook" program for charter vessel/guided catches of King Salmon in Southeast Alaska by the 1998 season.

Alaska

State and Federal Agencies

Alaska Dept. of Fish & Game
PO Box 25556
Juneau, AK 99802-5526
phone: (907) 465-4100

Alaska Region Forest Service
709 West 9th Street
Box 21628
Juneau, AK 99802-1628
phone: (907) 586-8863
TTY: (907) 586-7816

Chugach National Forest
3301 C Street, Ste. 300
Anchorage, AK 99503-3998
phone: (907) 271-2500
TTY: (907) 271-2332

Tongass National Forest:
Chatham Area
204 Siginaka Way
Sitka, AK 99835
phone: (907) 747-6671
TTY: (907) 747-8840

Bureau of Land Management
Alaska State Office
222 W. 7th Avenue, #13
Anchorage, AK 99513-7599
phone: (907) 271-5960
or (907) 271-plus extension
fax: (907) 271-4596

Office Hours: 7:30 a.m. - 4:15 p.m.

National Parks

Denali National Park
phone: (907) 683-2294

Gates of the Arctic National Park
phone: (907) 456-0281

Glacier Bay National Park
phone: (907) 697-2230

Katmai National Park
phone: (907) 246-3305

Kenai Fjords National Park
phone: (907) 224-3175

Kobuk Valley National Park
phone: (907) 442-3890

Lake Clark National Park
phone: (907) 271-3751

Wrangell-St. Elias National Park

Associations, Publications, etc.

North America Gamebird Association
1214 Brooks Avenue
Raleigh, NC 27607
email: gamebird@naga.org

Eagles' Ridge Ranch

Mike Crouch

HC 62, Box 5780 • Delta Junction, AK 99737
phone: (907) 895-4329 • fax: (907) 895-5252

Eagles' Ridge Ranch offers upland bird hunting on 2,800 acres of secluded timber, grassland, cropland and rolling hills in the heart of Alaska's interior from April through October. Hunt pheasants, chukars or quail released exclusively for our customers, or try your luck on sharptail, spruce or ruffed grouse, Canada and white-fronted geese, or sandhill cranes in season.

Use your own dog, or hire one of our knowledgeable guides and well-trained dogs to make the most of your upland hunting experience.

We offer several sporting clay ranges to sharpen your shooting skills, and hot, home-style meals served in the warm atmosphere and country charm of our clubhouse.

"Friendly, well prepared, relaxed and not pushy but extremely productive. The best 'kick back' hunt I've ever enjoyed." R. Ruchong

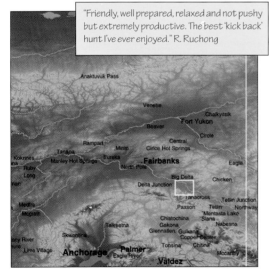

Picked-By-You Professionals in
Colorado

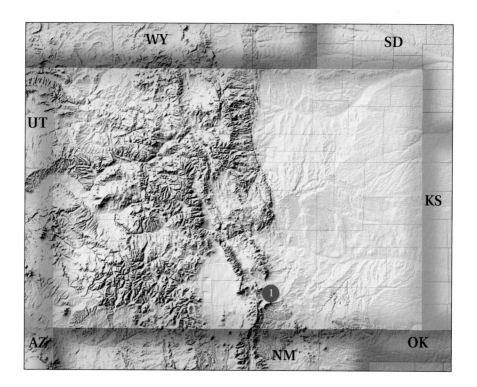

Outdoor Professionals

1 Echo Canyon Outfitters

License and Report Requirements

• State requires licensing of Outdoor Professionals.

• State requires an "Inter-Office Copy of Contract with Client" be submitted each time a client goes with an Outfitter. Colorado Agencies of Outfitters Registry sends this copy to client to fill out and return to their agency.

Useful information for the state of

Colorado

State and Federal Agencies

Colorado Agencies of Outfitters Registry
1560 Broadway, Suite 1340
Denver, CO 80202
phone: (303) 894-7778

Colorado Dept. of Natural Resources
1313 Sherman, Room 718
Denver, CO 80203
phone: (303) 866-3311

Forest Service
Rocky Mountain Region
740 Simms Street
PO Box 25127
Lakewood, CO 80225
phone: (303) 275-5350
TTY: (303) 275-5367

Arapaho-Roosevelt National Forests
Pawnee National Grassland
phone: (970) 498-2770

Grand Mesa-Umcompahgre
Gunnison National Forests
phone: (970) 874-7641

Pike-San Isabel National Forests
Commanche & Cimarron National
Grasslands
phone: (719) 545-8737

San Juan-Rio Grande National Forest
phone: (719) 852-5941

White River National Forest
phone: (970) 945-2521

Bureau of Land Management
Colorado State Office
2850 Youngfield St.
Lakewood, Co. 80215-7093
phone: (303) 239-3600
fax: (303) 239-3933
Tdd: (303) 239-3635

Email: msowa@co.blm.gov

Office Hours: 7:45 a.m. - 4:15 p.m.

National Parks

Mesa Verde National Park, CO 81330
phone: (303) 529-4465

Rocky Mountain National Park
phone: (303) 586-2371

Associations, Publications, etc.

Colorado Outfitters Association
PO Box 1304
Parker, CO 80134
phone: (303) 841-7760

International Hunter Education Assoc
PO Box 347
Jamestown, CO 80455
phone: (303) 449-0631
fax: (303) 449-0576

Rocky Mountain Bighorn Society
PO Box 8320
Denver, CO 80201

Echo Canyon Outfitters

David Hampton

P.O. Box 328 • La Veta, CO 81055
phone: (800) 341-6603 • (719) 742-5524 • fax: (719) 742-5525
email: echo@rmi.net • www.guestecho.com • Lic. #1143

Echo Canyon Outfitters provides first-class trophy- quality hunts on a private ranch. Our hunters are guided one-on-one by experienced guides who are very knowledgeable of the terrain and wildlife. The hunts are extremely professional, offering quality accommodations, food, stock, and personnel.

We are active members of Rocky Mountain Elk Foundation as sponsors, donors and habitat partners. Our Long Canyon Ranch is strictly managed for wildlife habitat and trophy-class production under a conservation easement with RMEF. The outfit brings 12 years' of solid experience to our business.

We annually re-book more than 75% of our clients two years in advance. We specialize in trophy elk and mule deer, black bear, mountain lion and <u>turkey</u>.

"Echo Canyon Outfitters are very professional yet they treat you like family. They go out of their way to ensure you a memorable experience."

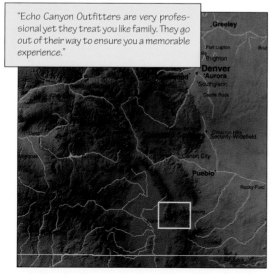

Idaho

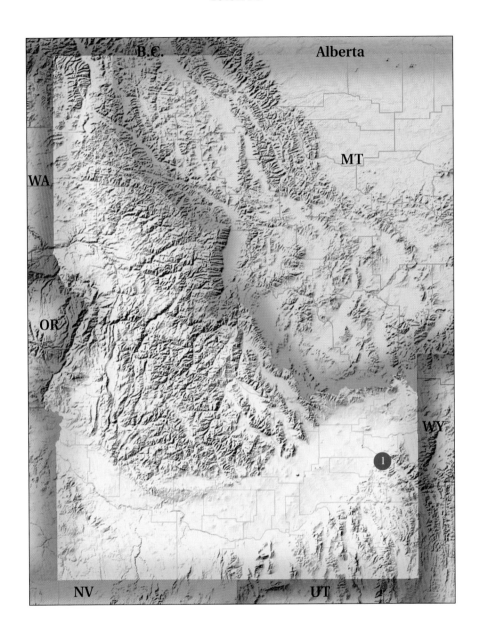

Outdoor Professionals

1 Wapiti River Guides

Useful information for the state of
Idaho

State and Federal Agencies

Outfitter & Guides Licensing Board
1365 N. Orchard, Room 172
Boise, ID 83706
phone: (208) 327-7380
fax: (208) 327-7382

Idaho Fish & Game Dept.
600 South Walnut
Boise, ID 83707
phone: (208) 334-3700

Forest Service
Northern Region
Federal Bldg.
PO Box 7669
Missoula, MT 59807-7669
phone: (406) 329-3616
TTY: (406) 329-3510

Clearwater National Forest
phone: (208) 476-4541

Idaho Panhandle, Coeur d'Alene-
Kaniksu-St. Joe National Forests
phone / TTY: (208) 765-7223

Nez Perce National Forest
phone: (208) 983-1950

Bureau of Land Management
Idaho State Office
1387 S. Vinnell Way
Boise, ID 83709-1657
phone: (208) 373-3896
or (208) 373-plus extension
fax: (208) 373-3899

Office Hours 7:45 a.m. - 4:15 p.m.

Associations, Publications, etc.

North America Gamebird Association
1214 Brooks Avenue
Raleigh, NC 27607
email: gamebird@naga.org

Idaho Outfitters & Guides Association
PO Box 95
Boise, ID 83701
phone: (208) 342-1438

License and Report Requirements

• State requires licensing of Outdoor Professionals.

• State requires that every Outfitter be it bird, fish, big game, river rafting, trail riding or packing file a "Use Report" annually.

• Currently, no requirements for Guest/Dude Ranches.

Wapiti River Guides

Gary Lane

P.O. Box 1125 • Riggins, ID 83549
phone: (800) 488-9872 • (208) 628-3523 • fax: (208) 628-3523
email: wapitirg@cyberhighway.net

Float Idaho's Salmon River by driftboat for chukar hunting and steelhead fishing combination trips. Flowing through the second deepest gorge in North America, the river will introduce you to steep, rugged terrain.

After traversing the breathtaking terra firma with your dog (if you like), come back to the boats and relax with a fishing rod in your hands — that is, until a magnificent red-sided steelhead takes your line into the sky.

We place two clients per driftboat and send a baggage boat and crew ahead to secure camps, which allows us more time to hunt and fish between destinations.

Trips range from one to six days. Chukar/steelhead trips are offered only on the Salmon River. Steelhead fishing is offered on both the Salmon and Oregon's Grande Ronde River, a fly fishermen's paradise. Whitewater and scenic trips are also offered.

Iowa

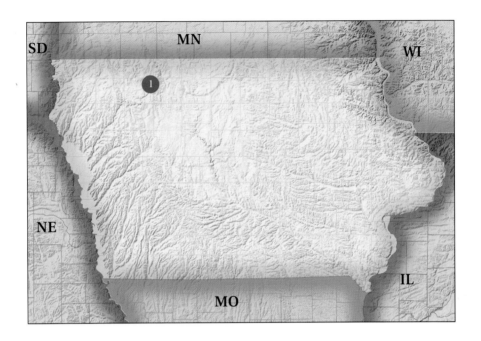

Outdoor Professionals

 Sure Shot Guide Service

Useful information for the state of
Iowa

State and Federal Agencies

Dept. of Natural Resources
East 9th & Grand Avenue
Wallace Building
Des Moines, IA 50319
(515) 281-5918

Bureau of Land Management
Eastern States
7450 Boston Boulevard
Springfield, Virginia 22153
phone: (703) 440-1660
or (703) 440-plus extension
fax: (703) 440-1599

Office Hours: 8:00 a.m. - 4:30 p.m.

Eastern States
Milwaukee District Office
310 W. Wisconsin Ave., Suite 450
(P.O. Box 631 53201-0631)
Milwaukee, Wisconsin 53203
phone: (414) 297-4450
fax: (414) 297-4409

Associations, Publications, etc.

North America Gamebird Association
1214 Brooks Avenue
Raleigh, NC 27607
email: gamebird@naga.org

License and Report Requirements

• State does not license or register Outfitters, Guides or Lodges.

• State has no report requirements.

Sure-Shot Guide Service

Don Nolan

1210 Gordon Drive, P.O. Box 889 • Okoboji, IA 51355-0889

phone: (712) 332-9107 • fax: (712) 338-2263

We are northwest Iowa's first and best guide service. We offer more than 50 years' of combined hunting experience in the pheasant capital of the U.S. Hunters are welcome on the farms and are treated with utmost hospitality. Wild birds under wild conditions are our specialty. We can handle large groups or just a one-person hunt. We hunt cornfields, beanfields, groves, railroad tracks, dredge ditches, fencelines, road ditches and terraces. We also offer waterfowl and combination upland and waterfowl hunts.

We also have dog training available from start to finish, and a place to clean your birds and keep your dogs. We're designed by hunters for hunters. References furnished on request.

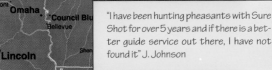

"I have been hunting pheasants with Sure Shot for over 5 years and if there is a better guide service out there, I have not found it" J. Johnson

Kansas

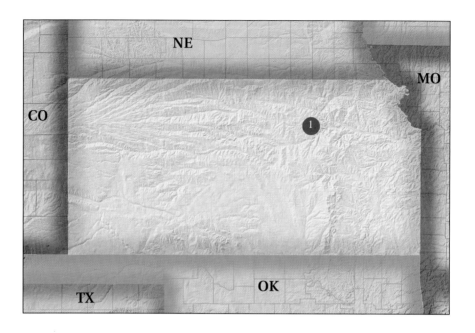

<u>Outdoor Professionals</u>

1 Prairie Winds Guide Service

Useful information for the state of

Kansas

State and Federal Agencies

Kansas Dept. of Wildlife & Parks
900 SW Jackson St., Suite 502
Topeka, KS 66612
phone: (913) 296-2281
fax: (913) 296-6953

Bureau of Land Management
New Mexico State Office
(serves Kansas, Oklahoma & Texas)
Street Address:
1474 Rodeo Road
Santa Fe, NM 87505

Mailing Address:
P.O. Box 27115
Santa Fe, NM 87502-0115
Information Number: (505) 438-7400
fax: (505) 438-7435
Public Lands Information Center (PLIC):
(505) 438-7542

Office Hours: 7:45 a.m. - 4:30 p.m.

Associations, Publications, etc.

North America Gamebird Association
1214 Brooks Avenue
Raleigh, NC 27607
email: gamebird@naga.org

License and Report Requirements
• State requires a Guide license for Hunting and Fishing.

• State requires that a "Fish-Hunt Guides Annual Report" be filed by January 15th
  each year.

Prairie Winds Guide Service

Tom Slick

1611 K-157 Highway • Junction City, KS 66441
phone: (913) 257-3234

Situated on the western edge of the famous Flint Hills in the north-central Kansas, Prairie Winds Guide Service is ideally located to provide hunters and anglers almost everything that Kansas has to offer.

Upland game, whitetail deer and turkey are plentiful. If you are looking for fishing or waterfowl hunting, we are surrounded by four major lakes plus several city and county lakes and numerous farm ponds where the bass fishing is awesome.

All of our upland bird hunts are for wild birds that test you and your dogs' abilities. We hunt from dawn until sundown unless otherwise agreed on. We have several excellent dogs to supplement yours at no extra charge. Tom has hunting rights to several private farms in the countryside surrounding Junction City, and offers challenging shooting for all wild birds.

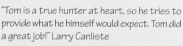

"Tom is a true hunter at heart, so he tries to provide what he himself would expect. Tom did a great job!" Larry Canliste

Maine

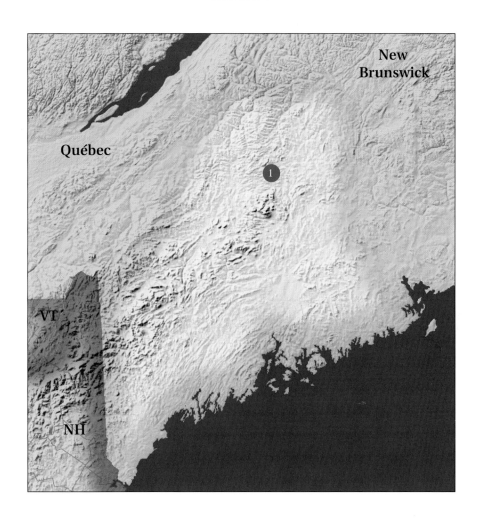

Outdoor Professionals

1 Libby Sporting Camps

Useful information for the state of
Maine

State and Federal Agencies

Maine Dept. of Fish & Wildlife
284 State St. Station #41
Augusta, ME 04333
phone: (207) 287-8000

Forest Service
Eastern Region
310 West Wisconsin Ave. Rm. 500
Milwaukee, WI 53203
phone: (414) 297-3646
TTY: (414) 297-3507

White Mountain National Forest
Federal Building
719 North Main Street
Laconia, NH 03246
phone: (603) 528-8721

Bureau of Land Management
Eastern States
7450 Boston Boulevard
Springfield, Virginia 22153
phone: (703) 440-1660
or (703) 440- Plus Extension
fax: (703) 440-1599

Office Hours: 8:00 a.m. - 4:30 p.m.

Eastern States
Milwaukee District Office
310 W. Wisconsin Ave., Suite 450

(P.O. Box 631 53201-0631)
Milwaukee, Wisconsin 53203
phone: (414) 297-4450
fax: (414) 297-4409

National Parks

Acadia National Park
phone: (207) 288-3338

Associations, Publications, etc.

North America Gamebird Association
1214 Brooks Avenue
Raleigh, NC 27607
email: gamebird@naga.org

Sportsman's Alliance of Maine
RR 1, Box 1174
Church Hill Road
Augusta, ME 04330-9749
phone: (207) 622-5503

Maine Professional Guide Association
phone: (207) 785-2061

The Maine Sportsman
phone: (207) 287-3995

License and Report Requirements
• State requires licensing of Outdoor Professionals.

• Monthly Head Fee Guides Report required for Whitewater River Companies.

• No report required for Hunting and Fishing Professionals.

Libby Sporting Camps

Matthew and Ellen Libby

P.O. Box V, Dept. 0 • Ashland, ME 04732
radio phone: (207) 435-8274 • fax: (207) 435-3230
email: libbycam@libbycam.sdi.agate.net

The Libby family has operated a lodge and guide service in the Aroostook and Allagash River headwaters of Maine since 1890. The camp is located 150 miles north of Bangor in the heart of a 4-million acre wilderness near the Canadian border. Hunting for trophy deer, bear and moose is second to none in the state.

An abundance of grouse rounds out the hunter's dream.

The six guest cabins are comfortable, clean, spacious and private. The food is home-cooked and served family-style in the dining room overlooking the lake. The cabins are handcrafted — from the peeled log timbers and immense fieldstone fireplace in the lodge to the handmade quilts on the beds. Perfect accommodations for families, business groups and honeymooners.

"One does not survive for 3+ generations in this business and NOT learn how things should be done. The Libby Family stands as a model for others to follow." Fitzhugh L. Brown

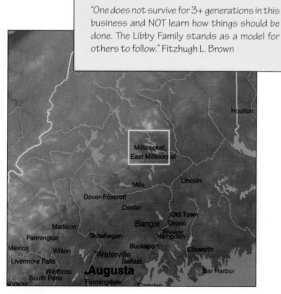

Mississippi

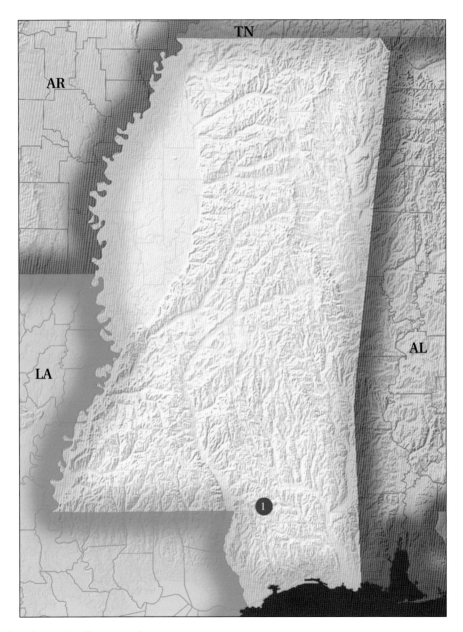

Outdoor Professionals

1 Longleaf Plantation

Useful information for the state of

Mississippi

State and Federal Agencies

Dept. of Wildlife, Fisheries & Parks
2906 North State St.
Jackson, MS
(601) 362-9212

Mississippi Division of Tourism
(800) 927-6378

Bureau of Land Management
Eastern States
7450 Boston Boulevard
Springfield, Virginia 22153
phone: (703) 440-1660
or (703) 440-plus extension
fax: (703) 440-1599

Office Hours: 8:00 a.m. - 4:30 p.m.

Eastern States
Jackson Field Office
411 Briarwood Drive, Suite 404
Jackson, Mississippi 39206
phone: (601) 977-5400
fax: (601) 977-5440

Forest Service
Southern Region
1720 Peachtree Road NW
Atlanta, GA 30367
phone: (404) 347-4177
TTY: (404) 347-4278

Bienville, Delta, DeSoto, Holly Springs,
Homochitto, and Tombigbee National
Forests
100 West Capitol St., Suite 1141
Jackson, MS 39269
phone /TTY: (601) 965-4391

Associations, Publications, etc.

North America Gamebird Association
1214 Brooks Avenue
Raleigh, NC 27607
email: gamebird@naga.org

Mississippi Outfitters & Guide Assoc.
(800) 777-4210

License and Report Requirements

• Currently, State does not license or register Outfitters, Captains, Guides or Lodges.

• Currently, State has no report requirements.

• Law Enforcement Division of Fisheries & Parks reports that Mississippi is in the process of developing law which will require state licensing for outfitters, definitely big game and will possibly include fishing, upland bird and waterfowl hunting. Due to take effect in 1998.

Longleaf Plantation

George Alexander

P.O. Box 511 • Lumberton, MS 39455

phone: (800) 421-7370 • (601) 794-6001 • fax: (601) 794-5052

In the lower region of the Mississippi is a 3,000 acre retreat called Longleaf Plantation, taking its name from the majestic stand of longleaf pines which are characteristic to the area. Longleaf Plantation embodies the very spirit of the Old South quail hunt, offering sport, superb accommodations, southern cuisine, and natural privacy.

To experience the hunt or just enjoy peaceful seclusion from "the outside world," guests arrive for a variety of reasons but leave fully-rested with renewed vigor.

This effect has expanded our clientele to include individuals as well as corporations who come to Longleaf for business and pleasure.

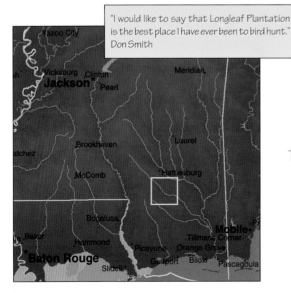

"I would like to say that Longleaf Plantation is the best place I have ever been to bird hunt."
Don Smith

Missouri

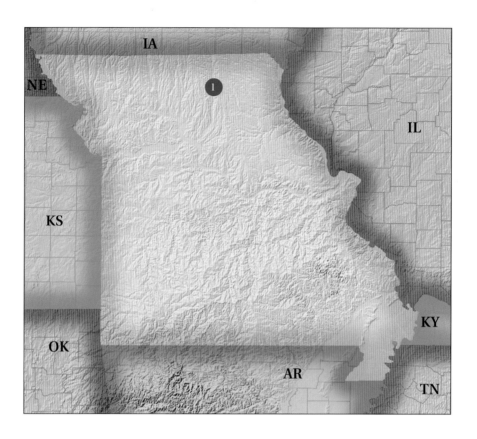

Outdoor Professionals

1 Farley's International Adventures

Missouri

State and Federal Agencies

Missouri Dept. of Conservation
PO Box 180
Jefferson City, MO 65102
phone: (573) 751-4115

Eastern Region National Forest
310 West Wisconsin Ave., Room 500
Milwaukee, WI 53203
phone: (414) 297-3646
TTY: (414) 297-3507

Mark Twain National Forest
401 Fairground Rd.
Rolla, MO 64501
phone/TTY: (573) 364-4621

Bureau of Land Management
Eastern States
7450 Boston Boulevard
Springfield, Virginia 22153
phone: (703) 440-1660
or (703) 440- Plus Extension
fax: (703) 440-1599

Office Hours: 8:00 a.m. - 4:30 p.m.

Eastern States
Milwaukee District Office
310 W. Wisconsin Ave., Suite 450
(P.O. Box 631 53201-0631)
Milwaukee, Wisconsin 53203
phone: (414) 297-4450
fax: (414) 297-4409

Associations, Publications, etc.

North America Gamebird Association
1214 Brooks Avenue
Raleigh, NC 27607
email: gamebird@naga.org

License and Report Requirements

• State does not license or register Outfitters, Guides, Captains or Lodges.

• State has no report requirements.

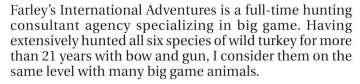

Farley's International Adventures

Bill Farley

Rt. 3, Box 13BB Tamarack Drive • Kirksville, MO 63501
phone/fax: (816) 665-4915

Farley's International Adventures is a full-time hunting consultant agency specializing in big game. Having extensively hunted all six species of wild turkey for more than 21 years with bow and gun, I consider them on the same level with many big game animals.

I have donated turkey hunts to fund-raisers for the National Wild Turkey Federation, Foundation for North American Wild Sheep, Safari Club International, Dallas Safari Club, and the North American Hunting Club. I am also an approved outfitter through the North American Hunting Clubs Outfitter Program. My operation prides itself on providing the best turkey hunt available under fair chase standards.

Clients praise us for our extra efforts. We offer the dedicated turkey hunter the best in turkey hunting on this continent, with our hunts in Missouri leading the way as "'the best of the best."

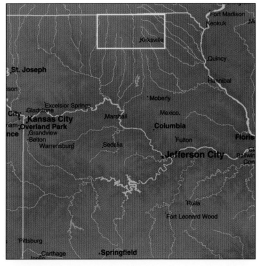

Montana

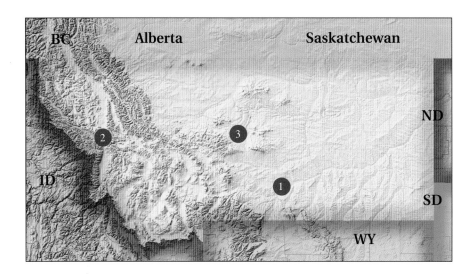

Outdoor Professionals

1. Eagle Nest Lodge & Outfitters
2. Good's Bird Hunts/Eagle Outfitters
3. Triple B Outfitters

Montana

State and Federal Agencies

Montana Board of Outfitters
Dept. of Commerce
Arcade Building - 111 North Jackson
Helena, MT 59620-0407
phone: (406) 444-3738

Montana Dept. of Fish, Wildlife & Parks
1420 East 6th
Helena, MT 59620
phone: (406) 444-2535

Forest Service
Northern Region
Federal Building
PO Box 7669
Missoula, MT 59807-7669
phone: (406) 329-3616
TTY: (406) 329-3510

Bitterroot National Forest
phone: (406) 363-7117

Custer National Forest
phone / TTY: (406) 657-6361

Flathead National Forest
phone: (406) 755-5401

Gallatin National Forest
phone / TTY: (406) 587-6920

Helena National Forest
phone: (406) 449-5201

Kootenai National Forest
phone: (406) 293-6211

Lewis & Clark National Forest
phone: (406) 791-7700

Lolo National Forest
phone: (406) 329-3750

Bureau of Land Management
Montana State Office
Granite Tower
222 North 32nd Street
P.O. Box 36800
Billings, Montana 59107-6800
phone: (406) 255-2885
fax: (406) 255-2762
Email - mtinfo@mt.blm.gov
Office Hours: 8:00 a.m. - 4:30 p.m.

National Parks

Glacier National Park
phone: (406) 888-5441

Associations, Publications, etc.

North America Gamebird Association
1214 Brooks Avenue
Raleigh, NC 27607
email: gamebird@naga.org

License and Report Requirements

• State requires licensing of Outdoor Professionals.

• State requires an "Annual Client Report Log" for all Hunting and Fishing Outfitters.

• State does not regulate River Guides.

• Guest/Dude Ranches need to get an Outfitter license only if they take guest to fish or hunt on land that they do not own.

Eagle Nest Lodge & Outfitters

Keith Kelly

P.O. Box 509 • Hardin, MT 59034

phone: (406) 665-3711 • fax: (406) 665-3712

Eagle Nest, secluded on the banks of the Bighorn River, was the first in the world to receive the Orvis endorsement for excellence in wing-shooting and service.

The lodging and dining are synonymous with excellence, and the hills, creeks and fields of south-central Montana provide premier habitat for some of the world's finest upland bird hunting. Pheasants, Hungarian partridge and sharptail grouse abound 35,000 acres of private land open to Eagle Nest guests. Hunts are conducted by professional guides using German shorthairs, Brittanies, and English pointers. The shooting is quite challenging but the birds are plentiful.

A family business since its conception in 1982, Eagle Nest is owned and managed by the Kellys.

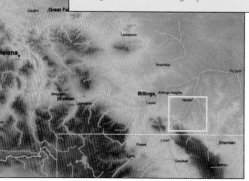

"I hunted for three days and I wish I had booked a longer trip. The area is beautiful and the birds were everywhere. Eagle Nest is a first class operation all the way from the dogs, to the birds, to the food." Jack Duley in "The Bird Hunting Report"

Good's Bird Hunts/Eagle Outfitters

Gerry Good

P.O. Box 1042 • Ravalli, MT 59863
phone/fax: (406) 745-3491
email: sti3491@Montana.com

Good's Bird Hunts is a small central Montana company, offering first-class upland bird hunts. We provide the client with room and board, guides, dogs, transportation, and preparation of birds for shipping. Our season runs from September to mid-December, but is usually over when the weather turns bad in mid-November.

Because bird populations vary year to year, we offer different locations for lodging, from first-class motels to ranch-style accommodations where we stay on the ranch with home-cooked meals and bunkhouse beds. Most lunches are in the field.

We use Griffon pointing dogs, or you can use your dogs in partnership with ours. Groups are limited to three per guide. Our package is a four-night, three-day hunt with meals starting on the first night. Airport pickups can be arranged at Billings and Great Falls or other airports.

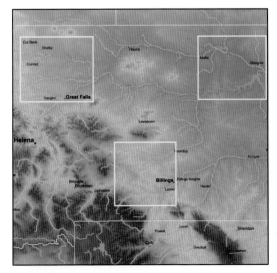

Triple B Outfitters

David L. Gill
616 W. Broadway • Lewistown, MT 59457
phone: (406) 538-2177

Central Montana is known nationwide for its excellent bird hunting due to the many different and abundant species of upland game birds. Hungarian partridge, sharptail grouse, ruffed grouse, blue grouse, sage hen and pheasant make for the finest in bird hunting.

If you would like to visit Montana and take part in some of the best bird hunting anywhere, we can arrange one- to five-day hunts for up to six people at a time.

We provide full guide service, transportation, access to quality private land with excellent bird populations, dogs and lunch in the field. You provide your own lodging, breakfast and dinner.

"He (Dave Gill) is a first class person, completely honest and capable of providing a very successful and enjoyable hunt. My son and I are waterfowl guides and outfitters. We know what it takes to provide a memorable hunt and Dave gives it all." *George Carr*

Nebraska

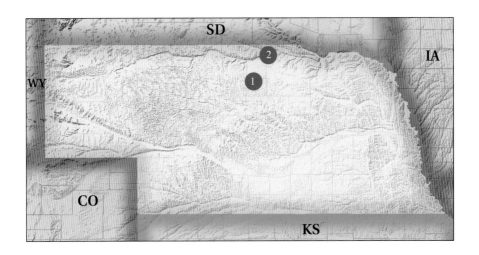

Outdoor Professionals

1. Sandhills Adventures
2. Wild Redheads Archery Turkey Hunts

Useful information for the state of
Nebraska

State and Federal Agencies

Nebraska Game & Parks Commission
Nebraska Fish & Game
2200 North 33rd Street
Lincoln, NE 68503
(402) 471-0641

Department of Tourism
(800) 658-4024

Bureau of Land Management
Wyoming State Office
(serves Nebraska also)
Information Access Center
5353 Yellowstone
P.O. Box 1828
Cheyenne, WY 82003
Phone: (307) 775-6BLM or 6256
FAX: (307) 775-6082

Office Hours: 7:45 a.m. - 4:30 p.m.

Forest Service
Rocky Mountain Region
740 Simms Street
PO Box 25127
Lakewood, CO 80225
phone: (303) 275-5350
TTY: (303) 275-5367

Ogala, Ft. Pierre and Buffalo Gap National
Grasslands
125 North Main Street
Chadron, NE 69337
phone: (308) 432-0300
TTY: (308) 432-0304

Associations, Publications, etc.

North America Gamebird Association
1214 Brooks Avenue
Raleigh, NC 27607
email: gamebird@naga.org

License and Report Requirements
• State does not license or register Outfitters, Captains, Guides or Lodges.

• State has no report requirements.

Sandhills Adventures

Dalton and Marilyn Rhoades

HC 63, Box 29 • Brewster, NE 68821
phone: (308) 547-2210 • fax: (308) 547-2228

Uncle Buck's Lodge invites you to experience the friendliest hospitality and most relaxing atmosphere you'll ever encounter. It overlooks the North Loup River at the edge of Brewster which, with a population of 22, is the smallest county seat in the nation.

We are located in the Sandhills of Nebraska where abundant lakes and rivers are fed by the Ogallala Aquifer. This water source is truly a miraculous phenomenon and is the basis for the region and state's wealth. These assets create wonderful waterfowl production. Prairie chickens, the rarest upland game bird in North America, isn't rare here. Pheasants, turkey, sharptail grouse, goose and duck are all plentiful. You'll hunt these birds on 200,000 acres of private ground with experienced guides and well-trained hunting dogs.

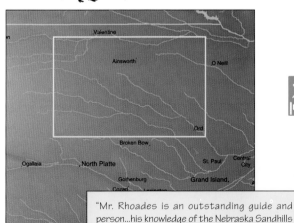

"Mr. Rhoades is an outstanding guide and person...his knowledge of the Nebraska Sandhills is outstanding... facilities and food are excellent. I highly recommend him and Sandhill Adventures"

Wild Redheads Archery Turkey Hunts

Jason Lambley

Box 586 • Fisher Branch, Manitoba, Canada R0C 0Z0
phone: (204) 372-6113 • fax: (204) 372-8435

Wild Redheads Archery Turkey Hunts, operated by Jason Lambley, offers a limited number of archery hunts each year for Merriam's turkeys in north-central Nebraska and southern South Dakota.

By using sophisticated hunting gear, such as battery-operated mounted hen and tom turkeys as decoys as well as custom-made blinds, enables hunters to shoot from 5 to 20 yards. This three-and-a-half-day hunt is as hard as the hunter desires; most days finds us in the field from morning until dark.

I truly believe that my determination and desire to succeed in anything that I undertake will find your hunt both successful and a lifetime memory.

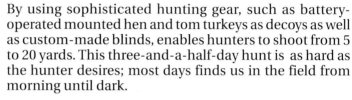

"It was such a good hunt that I am re-booking it every year!" Charles J. Davis

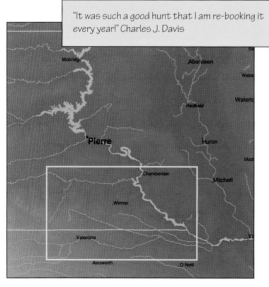

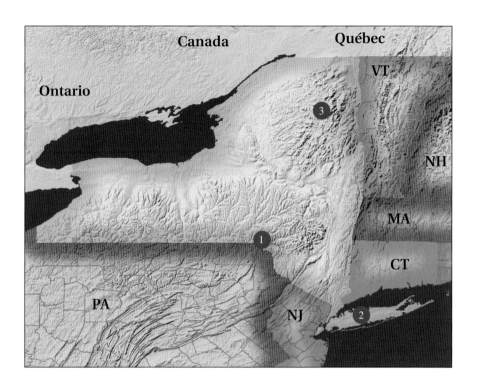

Outdoor Professionals

1. Catskill Pheasantry
2. DC Outdoor Adventures, Inc.
3. The Hungry Trout Motor Inn

Useful information for the state of
New York

State and Federal Agencies

Dept. of Environmental Conservation
50 Wolf Rd.
Albany, NY 12233
phone: (518) 457-3400

Bureau of Land Management
Eastern States
7450 Boston Boulevard
Springfield, Virginia 22153
phone: (703) 440-1660
or (703) 440- Plus Extension
fax: (703) 440-1599

Office Hours: 8:00 a.m. - 4:30 p.m.

Eastern States
Milwaukee District Office
310 W. Wisconsin Ave., Suite 450
(P.O. Box 631 53201-0631)
Milwaukee, Wisconsin 53203
phone: (414) 297-4450
fax: (414) 297-4409

Fire Island National Seashore
120 Laurel Street
Patchogue, NY 11772
phone: (516) 289-4810

Associations, Publications, etc.

North America Gamebird Association
1214 Brooks Avenue
Raleigh, NC 27607
email: gamebird@naga.org

New York State Outdoor Guides Assoc.
(NYSOGA)
PO Box 4704
Queensbury, NY 12804
phone/fax: (518) 798-1253

License and Report Requirements
• State requires licensing of Guides.

• State requires that Guides be re-certified each year.

• State has no report requirements.

Catskill Pheasantry

Alex and Jill Papp

P.O. Box 42 • Long Eddy, NY 12760
phone: (914) 887-4487 • fax: (914) 887-4490
email: bang@zelacom.com

Our hunting preserve is located in the scenic foothills of the Catskill Mountains. The preserve, established in 1981, offers 450 acres of woods, streams, fields and the finest flight-conditioned pheasants and chukars. We have extensively planted fields to provide a natural and challenging hunt.

We offer bed and breakfast and will dress your birds for your trip home. Hunters with their own dog receive a discount.

Open seven days a week September through March.

"The fact that they are so close to New York City makes it unbelievable... It's like a western experience. I plan on going many more times with my Grandson!" Douglas Spolestra

D.C. Outdoor Adventures, Inc.

Capt. Dennis Caracciolo
P.O. Box 2187 • Brentwood, NY 11717
phone: (516) 231-0566 • beeper: (516) 834-9858

I run a full-service guiding outfit. We hunt and fish for all species in season. My area of coverage is the entire eastern half of New York state from the Adirondacks to the Catskills, Hudson Valley and Long Island.

Waterfowl is hunted primarily on Long Island's north and south shores. A variety of species offer good shooting. Geese are hunted in September.

I hunt pheasant upstate during October with bonus grouse, woodcock and rabbits. Trained German shorthaired pointers are used.

Turkey is hunted in the fall and spring in central New York with good success.

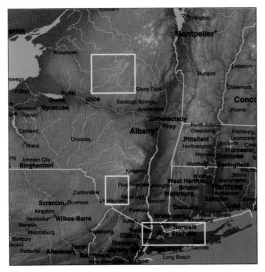

The Hungry Trout Motor Inn

Jerry and Linda Bottcher

Rt. 86 • Whiteface Mountain, NY 12997
phone: (800) 766-9137 • (518) 946-2217 • fax: (518) 946-7418
email: hungrytrout@whiteface.net • www.hungrytrout.com

The Hungry Trout Motor Inn rests on the banks of the legendary West Branch of the Ausable River in New York's Adirondack Mountains. Fifteen minutes from Lake Placid, The Hungry Trout has been headquarters for anglers and bird hunters wishing upscale lodging, gourmet dining and access to private water and superb grouse hunting. The Hungry Trout Fly Shop is a leading outfitter in the area and offers professional fishing and grouse hunting guide service throughout the season.

Starting in late fall, you can combine trout fishing and grouse hunting on the same day as the Adirondacks harbor some of the best grouse cover in New York State. The Inn has first-class packages that combine lodging, dining and guide service.

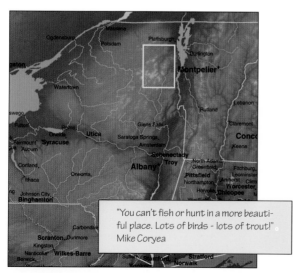

"You can't fish or hunt in a more beautiful place. Lots of birds - lots of trout!"
Mike Coryea

Picked-By-You Professionals in
North Dakota

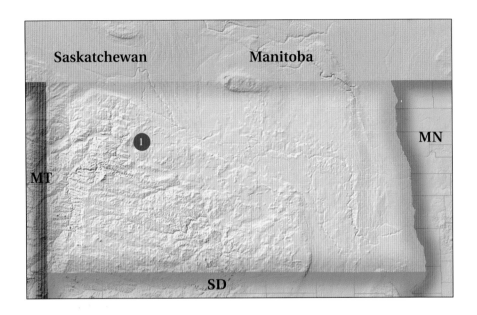

Outdoor Professionals

 Hap's Guide Service

Useful information for the state of
North Dakota

State and Federal Agencies

North Dakota Game & Fish Dept.
100 North Bismarck Expressway
Bismarck, ND 58501
phone: (701) 328-6300
fax: (701) 328-6352

Bureau of Land Management
Montana State Office
(serves North & South Dakota also)
222 North 32nd Street
P.O. Box 36800
Billings, MT 59107-6800

phone: (406) 255-2885
fax: (406) 255-2762
email - mtinfo@mt.blm.gov

Dakotas District Office
2933 Third Avenue West
Dickinson, ND 58601-2619

phone: (701) 225-9148
fax: (701) 227-8510
email - ddomail@mt.blm.gov

Office Hours: 8:00 a.m. - 4:30 p.m.

State Forest Service
307 First Street
Bottineau, ND 58318-1100
phone: (701) 228-5422
fax: (701) 228-5448

National Parks

Theodore Roosevelt National Park
Medora, ND 58645
phone: (701) 623-4466

Associations, Publications, etc.

North America Gamebird Association
1214 Brooks Avenue
Raleigh, NC 27607
email: gamebird@naga.org

Dakota Outdoors
PO Box 669
Pierre, SD 57501-0669
phone: (605) 224-7301
fax: (605) 224-9210

License and Report Requirements
• State does not license or register Outfitters, Guides, or Lodges.

• State has no report requirements.

Hap's Guide Service

Box 1024 • Garrison, ND 58540
phone: (701) 463-2084

In the fall of the year the Garrison, North Dakota-area abounds with waterfowl for the avid hunter. First to migrate are the sandhill cranes in mid-September followed by Canada honkers and northern mallards in October.

Many potholes in the area raise local broods of ducks and Canada geese. Except for hunting the potholes for ducks, geese and cranes are hunted on wheat, barley, and oat stubblefields. All hunts are over decoys and many days ducks are taken while hunting cranes or geese. Field blinds are provided, which are heated when temperatures fall. Bird cleaning, packaging, and freezing are available locally.

Motel lodging is available locally as are restaurants and a supper club.

"Hap is a very good guide...always gets bird...good worker and fun to be with!"
Bob Hennen

Picked-By-You Professionals in
Pennsylvania

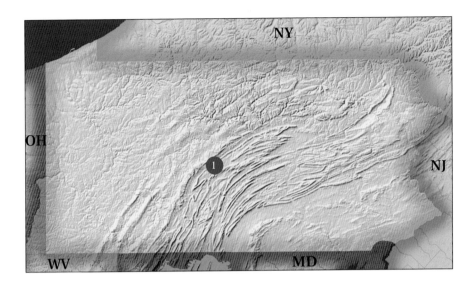

Outdoor Professionals

1 Warriors Mark Shooting Preserve

Useful information for the state of

Pennsylvania

State and Federal Agencies

Pennsylvania Game Commission
2001 Elmerton Ave.
Harrisburg, PA 17110
hunting: (717) 787-4250
fishing: (717) 657-4518

Division of Tourism
Commonwealth of Pennsylvania
phone: (800) 847-4872

Forest Service
Eastern Region
310 West Wisconsin Avenue, Room 500
Milwaukee, WI 53203
phone: (414) 297-3646
TTY: (414) 297-3507

Allegheny National Forest
222 Liberty Street
PO Box 847
Warren, PA 16365
phone: (814) 723-5150
TTY: (814) 726-2710

Bureau of Land Management
Eastern States
7450 Boston Boulevard
Springfield, Virginia 22153
phone: (703) 440-1660
or (703) 440- Plus Extension
fax: (703) 440-1599

Office Hours: 8:00 a.m. - 4:30 p.m.

Eastern States
Milwaukee District Office
310 W. Wisconsin Ave., Suite 450
(P.O. Box 631 53201-0631)
Milwaukee, Wisconsin 53203
phone: (414) 297-4450
fax: (414) 297-4409

Associations, Publications, etc.

North America Gamebird Association
1214 Brooks Avenue
Raleigh, NC 27607
email: gamebird@naga.org

The Ruffed Grouse Society
451 McCormick Road
Coraopolis, PA 15108
phone: (412) 262-4044

License and Report Requirements
• State requires licensing of Outdoor Professionals.

• State requires the filing of the "Charter Boat/Fishing Guide Report".

Warriors Mark Shooting Preserve

Eric Gilliland

RD 1, Box 464 • Warriors Mark, PA 16877
phone: (814) 632-6680 • fax: (814) 632-3072

Warriors Mark Shooting Preserve, Kennels and Archery is located in the heart of central Pennsylvania's Appalachian Mountains. The preserve consists of more than 1,000 acres of prime hunting grounds for pheasant, chukar, Hungarian partridge and quail with excellent cover, ranging from grain plots, weedlots and open fields to heavy brush and deep woods. Various packages are available and we provide setups for corporate outings and tournaments.

We offer a wide range of year-round dog training programs individually tailored to suit your needs. Our heated and air controlled 1,000 square foot kennel provides a secure, clean and friendly environment for your dog. The preserve also includes a 21 lane indoor archery range, an outdoor Known Distance Range, and various 3D ranges. A 5,000 square foot clubhouse includes a lounge, pro shop, meeting and banquet facilities and guest quarters.

"Warriors Mark is an excellent facility for field and continental pheasant hunts. Plenty of action! Management & staff are excellent" Robert R. Spaulding

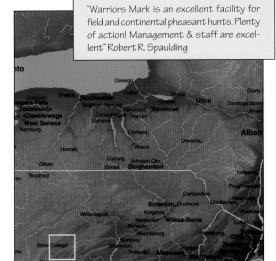

South Dakota

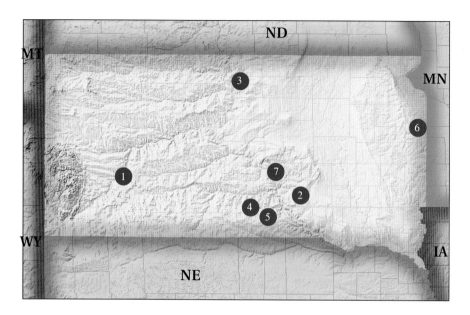

Outdoor Professionals

1. Cow Creek Ranch
2. Don Reeves Pheasant Ranch
3. Missouri River Ringnecks
4. P & R Hunting Lodge
5. S & S Hunting Service
6. South Dakota Pheasant Hunts
7. Willow Creek Wildlife, Inc.

Useful information for the state of

South Dakota

State and Federal Agencies

South Dakota Game & Fish Dept.
523 East Capitol
Pierre, SD 57501
phone: (605) 773-3381

Bureau of Land Management
Montana State Office
(serves North & South Dakota also)
222 North 32nd Street
P.O. Box 36800
Billings, MT 59107-6800

phone: (406) 255-2885
fax: (406) 255-2762
email - mtinfo@mt.blm.gov

Dakotas District Office
2933 Third Avenue West
Dickinson, ND 58601-2619

phone: (701) 225-9148
fax: (701) 227-8510
email - ddomail@mt.blm.gov

Office Hours: 8:00 a.m. - 4:30 p.m.

State Forest Service
Rocky Mountain Region
740 Simms Street
PO Box 25127
Lakewood, CO 80225
phone: (303) 275-5350
TTY: (303) 275-5367

Black Hills National Forest
Rt. 2, Box 200
Custer, SD 57730
phone: (605) 673-2251
TTY: (605) 673-4954

National Parks

Wind Cave National Park
Hot Springs, SD 57747

Badlands National Park
PO Box 6
Interior, SD 57750
phone: (605) 433-5361

Associations, Publications, etc.

North America Gamebird Association
1214 Brooks Avenue
Raleigh, NC 27607
email: gamebird@naga.org

Dakota Outdoors
PO Box 669
Pierre, SD 57501-0669
phone: (605) 224-7301
fax: (605) 224-9210

License and Report Requirements

• State does not license or register Outfitters, Guides, or Lodges.

• State has no report requirements.

• Outfitters and Guides must file a "Sales Tax License" with the Dept. of Revenue.

Cow Creek Ranch

Glendon and Pam Shearer and Family

HCR 3, Box 12 • Wall, SD 57790

phone: (605) 279-2681

Cow Creek Ranch is a family-owned and operated working ranch, consisting of 7,000 acres of rugged river breaks. The ranch is bordered by the beautiful Cheyenne River.

Cow Creek Ranch offers meals, lodging and hunts for prairie merriam turkeys (which, after 10 years, we are still 100% successful), archery deer, mostly mule deer, coyotes, prairie dogs, grouse, pheasant and antelope. We even do some ranch vacations for those folks that just want to experience real ranch life in the Old West.

The Shearer family is very active in rodeos, ranching and movies. Several of the wagons in "Dances with Wolves" and many other movies were furnished by the Shearer Ranches. With all of the ranch activity, beautiful country and wildlife, your stay with the Shearers is likely to be an experience you'll never forget.

"If you want a trophy tom they will see that you have the opportunity" Cy Roth

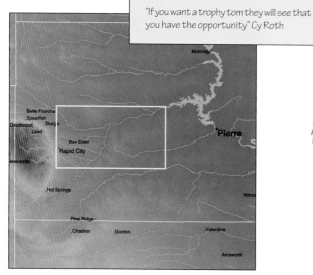

Don Reeves Pheasant Ranch

Don Reeves
Rt. 2, Box 30 • White Lake, SD 57383
phone: (605) 249-2693

Don Reeves Pheasant ranch is a working farm, located less than two hours from Sioux Falls. Several hundred acres of cornfields provide favorite cover for pheasants. Shelterbelts and fence rows also provide other places for pheasants to hide. You will hunt our birds just like you might hunt a farmer's cornfields, only you will see pheasants. In fact, we guarantee your limit.

Our birds aren't gathered around feeders or thrown from towers; they live in our cornfields, they run from the dogs or hold tight and take off with a cackle and a heart-stopping blur.

Don personally directs most of the hunting. With small groups, we hunt in the traditional method of drivers and blockers.

" A fun hunt with lots of chances for everyone" Charles Quarter

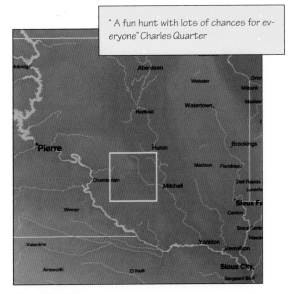

Missouri River Ringnecks

Marvin Schlomer

P.O. Box 158 • Glenham, S.D. 57631

phone: (888) 241-2280 • (605) 762-3325 • fax: (605) 762-3353

Experience the hunt of a lifetime in nature's heartland. The Missouri River Basin of northern South Dakota offers a plenitude of ringneck pheasants and other wild game in their natural habitat.

Missouri River Ringnecks' hunting area includes thousands of acres of prime wildlife habitat, including more than 1,000 acres of land in the Conservation Reserve Program, which fosters development of the wild game population, and cropland featuring native grasses, stubble, cornfields and sloughs. Not only do we provide excellent hunting ground for pheasants, but we also have a plentiful population of sharptail grouse, dove and trophy deer.

We offer more than 40,000 acres of scenic river breaks with cover for game birds and big game.

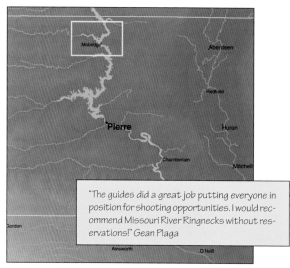

"The guides did a great job putting everyone in position for shooting opportunities. I would recommend Missouri River Ringnecks without reservations!" Gean Plaga

P & R Hunting Lodge

Paul and Ruth Taggart

Rt. 5, Box 117 • Dallas, SD 57529
phone: (605) 835-8050

It seems everyone who has been here can't wait for another year to roll around. The south-central part of South Dakota has long been the main pheasant hunting belt in the state and P & R Hunting Lodge, a 20,000 acre, family-owned operation, is located in the heart of the Golden Triangle. Starting in 1964, we were the first in South Dakota to go to a commercial operation.

We have followed a pheasant management program through three generations of farming and leave thousands of acres for pheasant habitat.

Our motto is, "Eat, sleep and hunt in one location." We provide guided hunts, home-cooked meals and facilities for cleaning and freezing birds. In the evening, all hunters gather for dinner at the Ringneck Saloon. Three-, five- and seven-day hunting packages are available.

"The Taggerts are very friendly and try to make your stay enjoyable. I just love that part of the country and the people!" Dale Lenoir

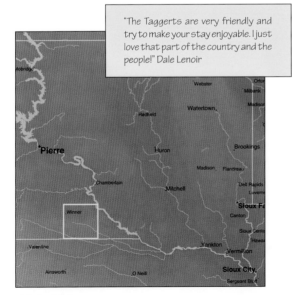

S & S Hunting Service

Gary and Mary Ann Shaffer

RR-1, Box 64 • Burke, SD 57523
phone: (605) 775-2262

Autumn in South Dakota is a hunter's paradise. South central South Dakota is commonly known as the "Pheasant Capital of the World," and our farm is located on hundreds of acres of prime hunting ground. We have been in the hunting business since 1983 and offer the finest old-fashioned ringneck hunting in South Dakota. Years of farming for wildlife has resulted in tremendous bird numbers.

We also provide seasonal combination hunts for grouse, prairie chicken, quail, dove, turkey, deer, goose and prairie dogs. The hunting package includes great guided hunts, modern lodging at our farm, tasty home-cooked meals, bird processing, and friendly, courteous service.

We strive to provide a great safe hunt, clean comfortable lodging and unsurpassed camaraderie.

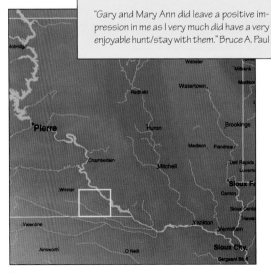

"Gary and Mary Ann did leave a positive impression in me as I very much did have a very enjoyable hunt/stay with them." Bruce A. Paul

South Dakota Pheasant Hunts

Will Stone

RR 1, Box 260 • Gary, SD 57237
phone: (800) 251-4198 • phone/fax: (605) 272-5608

Our hunts are the kind people have come to expect from South Dakota. You will hunt land that has been in the family for over 40 years. Throughout the years, the farm has been managed with wildlife in mind.

We welcome single hunters or groups. Although we provide dogs, your dogs are welcome. Our guides do not carry guns. You're paying for a good hunt, so we leave it up to you to bag the birds. Therefore, we can guarantee an ample population, but not limits. We do not over-book or combine hunting groups. We can clean, package and freeze your game after the hunt.

If you are not friends when you arrive, you will be when you leave. We look forward to serving you. Your success is our success.

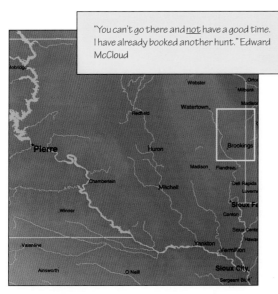

"You can't go there and not have a good time. I have already booked another hunt." Edward McCloud

Willow Creek Wildlife, Inc.

Steve and Bob Stoeser

20628 Willow Creek Rd. • Fort Pierre, SD 57532
phone: (800) 378-3154 • Steve: (605) 223-2079 • Bob: (605) 223-2933
email: clay@iw.net

You'll wake up to some of the best South Dakota scenery located right in the heart of pheasant country. Our hunting offers you pheasant, sharptail grouse, prairie chicken, goose, dove, whitetail and mule deer and antelope. Bird and big game hunts can be combined according to various seasons of each.

Our 13,000 acre hunting area includes a creek area with excellent cover for both birds and big game. Rolling prairie hills, wheat, corn and milo stubblefields provide good habitat and also attract geese from the Oahe Reservoir. We also hunt on native prairie grass. All hunts include guides, vehicles, gas and lunch.

We offer a very comfortable lodge located between our skeet and sporting clays course. The lodge will accommodate up to 10 people.

"Guaranteed great hunt in a relaxed, friendly atmosphere" Wendell Weakly

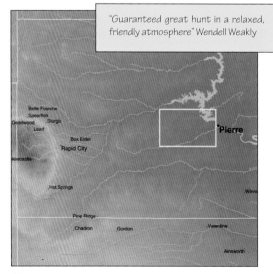

Texas

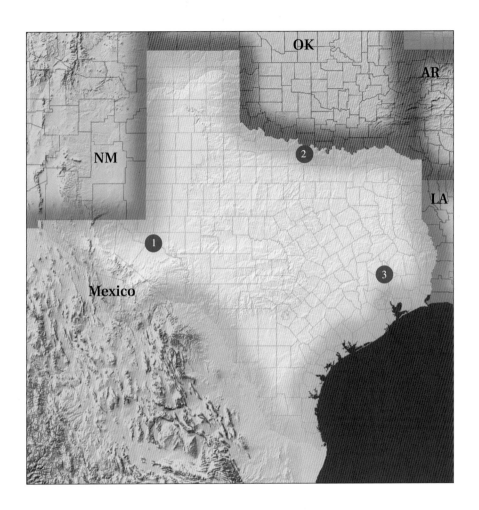

Outdoor Professionals

1. Adobe Lodge Hunting Camp
2. Game Management Services, Inc.
3. Palmetto Guide Service

Texas

State and Federal Agencies

Texas Parks & Wildlife Dept.
4200 Smith School Rd.
Austin, TX 78744
phone: (512) 389-4800

Texas Tourism
phone: (800) 888-8839

Forest Service
Southern Region
1720 Peachtree Road NW
Atlanta, GA 30367
phone: (404) 347-4177
TTY: (404) 347-4278

Angelina, Davy Crockett, Sabine, Sam
Houston National Forests
Homer Garrison Federal Bldg.
701 North First Street
Lufkin, TX 75901
phone/TTY: (409) 639-8501

Bureau of Land Management
New Mexico State Office
(serves Kansas, Oklahoma & Texas)
Street Address:
1474 Rodeo Road
Santa Fe, NM 87505

Mailing Address:
P.O. Box 27115
Santa Fe, NM 87502-0115

Information Number: (505) 438-7400
fax: (505) 438-7435
Public Lands Information Center (PLIC):
(505) 438-7542

Office Hours: 7:45 a.m. - 4:30 p.m.

National Parks

Big Bend National Park
Big Bend National Park, TX 79834
phone: (915) 477-2251

Guadalupe Mountains National Park
HC 60, Box 400
Salt Flat, TX 79847-9400
phone: (915) 828-3351

Associations, Publications, etc.

North America Gamebird Association
1214 Brooks Avenue
Raleigh, NC 27607
email: gamebird@naga.org

License and Report Requirements
• State does not license or register Outfitters, Guides, or Lodges.

• State has no report requirements.

Adobe Lodge Hunting Camp

Skipper Duncan

9660 US 67 South • San Angelo, TX 76904
ph. (915) 942-8040

Rookies and world-class veterans alike consistently describe their Adobe Lodge experience in the same way — their most FUN hunt ever.

You will hunt 100% private land which has a long tradition of super whitetail and turkey hunting.

Nationally known since 1987 as a hunting operation that has it all — good accommodations, good food, superb hunting and a well-run camp.

Adobe Lodge Hunting Camp enjoys a high level of repeat clients and word-of-mouth referrals.

Booking a hunt is easy — just call Skipper Duncan.

"The only BAD thing about this trip was when the tags ran out and it was time to go home."

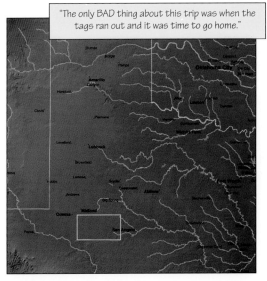

Game Management Services, Inc.

John A. Cox, President

P.O. Box 464 • Nocona, TX 76255
phone/fax: (940) 995-2210 • mobile/voice mail: (940) 736-4906
email: GmsInc84@aol.com

Game Management Services, Inc. was established in 1985 as a wildlife management and hunting organization, specializing in providing quality guided hunts to individuals and corporations. We have more than 150,000 acres of private land under lease in what many refer to as the last frontier for wild bird hunting. Our quail hunting operation has been featured in more than a dozen national magazines and outdoor publications.

We offer three-day or weekly hunt packages by foot, truck or horseback. We hunt with 40 fully-trained dogs — stylish pointers and setters.

Our hunts are exclusively for wild birds on some of the best quail country in North America.

"I can't say enough good about this trip. Guide's dogs were unbelievable - tremendous noses and stamina. Perfect manners on game." W.M. Cox, Fleetwood Farm

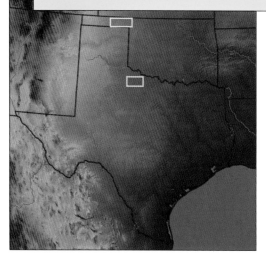

Palmetto Guide Service

Dave Scott Cox

65 Harmon Creek Ridge • Huntsville, TX 77340
phone: (409) 291-9602

Guide Dave Scott Cox, owner of Palmetto Guide Service, specializes in duck hunting, black bass and white bass fishing.

Duck hunts are fully-guided and semi-guided with boat transportation, trained retrievers, decoys and an experienced guide.

The area is in the heart of the central flyway where clients commonly harvest a variety of puddle ducks and diving ducks, with wood ducks, mallards and an occasional goose.

"David has the best dog I've ever hunted with and he (David) was very good at putting me on the birds." H. Willett

Washington

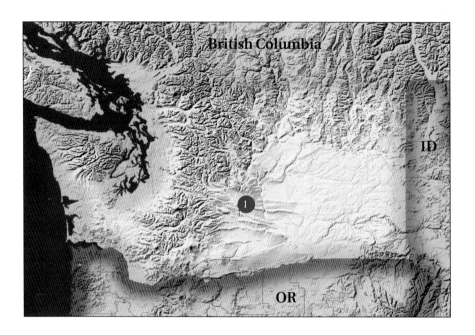

Outdoor Professionals

1 Reecer Creek Gamebird Ranch

Useful information for the state of
Washington

State and Federal Agencies

Washington Dept. of Wildlife
Licensing Division
600 North Capitol Way
Olympia, WA 98504
phone: (360) 902-2200

Forest Service
Pacific Northwest Region
333 SW 1st Avenue
PO Box 3623
Portland, OR 97208
phone: (503) 326-2971
TTY: (503) 326-6448

Colville National Forest
phone: (509) 684-7000

Gifford Pinchot National Forest
phone: (360) 750-5000

Mt. Baker-Snoqualmie National Forest
phone: (206) 775-9702

Okanogan National Forest
phone: (509) 826-3275

Wenatchee National Forest
phone: (509) 662-4335

Bureau of Land Management
Oregon State Office
(serves Washington also)
1515 SW 5th Ave.
P.O. Box 2965
Portland, OR 97208-2965
phone: (503) 952-6001
fax: (503) 952-6308

General Information:
or912mb@or.blm.gov
Webmaster: orwww@or.blm.gov
Office Hours: 7:30 a.m. - 4:30 p.m.

Spokane District Office
1103 N. Fancher
Spokane, WA 99212
phone: (509) 536-1200
fax: (509) 536-1275
E-mail: or130mb@or.blm.gov

National Parks

Mount Rainier NationalPark
phone: (206) 569-2211

North Cascades National Park
phone: (206) 856-5700

Olympic National Park
phone: (206) 452-4501

Associations, Publications, etc.

North America Gamebird Association
1214 Brooks Avenue
Raleigh, NC 27607
email: gamebird@naga.org

The Ptarmigans
PO Box 1821
Vancouver, WA 98668
phone: (206) 687-2436 / (206) 695-5385

Washington Outfitters & Guides Association
704 228th Avenue NE, Suite 331
Redmond, WA 98053
phone: (509) 674-5647

License and Report Requirements
• State requires licensing of Outdoor Professionals.
• State requires a "Fishing Guide Weekly Report".

Reecer Creek Gamebird Ranch

Claude Frable

463 Pheasant Lane • Ellensburg, WA 98926
phone: (800) 308-4868 • (509) 925-3781

Reecer Creek Gamebird Ranch is located in Central Washington on the edge of beautiful Kittitas Valley, 12 miles northwest of Ellensburg. The ranch features 800 acres of prime upland gamebird cover which is perfect for hunting of pheasant, quail and chukar. Fully-guided hunts and bird cleaning facilities are available.

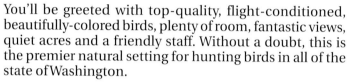

You'll be greeted with top-quality, flight-conditioned, beautifully-colored birds, plenty of room, fantastic views, quiet acres and a friendly staff. Without a doubt, this is the premier natural setting for hunting birds in all of the state of Washington.

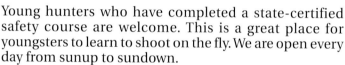

Young hunters who have completed a state-certified safety course are welcome. This is a great place for youngsters to learn to shoot on the fly. We are open every day from sunup to sundown.

"I recommend this hunting experience to anyone who trains dogs or just likes to hunt upland birds. It is also a great place to bring an inexperienced hunter." Dale Luther

Canada

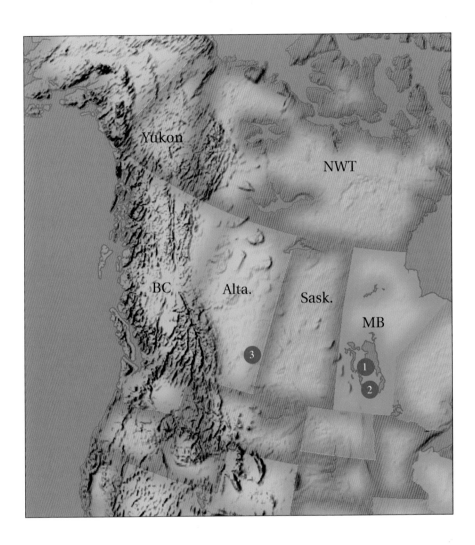

Outdoor Professionals

1. Big Antler Outfitters
2. Northern Honker Outfitters
3. Western Guiding Service

Canada

Alberta:
Ministries and Agencies

Dept. of Environmental Protection
9945-108 Street
Edmonton, Alberta, Canada T5K 2C6
phone: (403) 427-8636
fax: (403) 422-6339
email: Lfunke@env.gov.ab.ca

Natural Resources Service
9945-108 Street
Edmonton, Alberta, Canada T5K 2C6
phone: (403) 427-6749

Land and Forest Service
phone: (403) 427-3541

Associations, Publications, etc.

Ducks Unlimited Canada
#202, 10470-176 Street
Edmonton, Alberta, Canada T5S 1L3
phone: (403) 489-2002

North America Gamebird Association
1214 Brooks Avenue
Raleigh, NC 27607
email: gamebird@naga.org

Alberta Outfitters Association
Box 277
Caroline, Alberta, Canada T0K 0M0
phone/fax: (403) 722-2692

Professional Outfitters Association of
Alberta
PO Box 67012 Meadowlark Park
Edmonton, Alberta, Canada T5R 5Y3
phone: (403) 486-3050
fax: (403) 484-4942
The Outdoor Edge (publication)
5829-97 Street
Edmonton, Alberta, Canada T6E 3J2
phone: (403) 448-0381
fax: (403) 438-3244

Manitoba:
Ministries and Agencies

Department of Natural Resources
Legislative Building, Room 333
Winnipeg, MB Canada R3C 0V8
phone: (204) 945-3730

Dept. of Industry, Trade & Tourism
Travel Manitoba, Dept RH7
1515 Carlton St.
Winnipeg, MB Canada R3C 3H8
phone: (204) 945-3777/ext. RH7
fax: (204) 945-2302

Associations, Publications, etc.

Ducks Unlimited Canada
Box 1160
Sonewall, MB Canada R0C 2Z0
phone: (204) 467-3000
fax: (204) 467-9028

Delta Waterfowl Foundation
RR1, Box 1
Portage la Prairie, MB Canada R1N 3A1
phone: (204) 239-1900

North America Gamebird Association
1214 Brooks Avenue
Raleigh, NC 27607
email: gamebird@naga.org

Manitoba Lodges & Outfitters Assoc.
23 Sage Crescent
Winnipeg, MB Canada R2Y 0X8
phone: (204) 889-4840

Big Antler Outfitters

Ron Chekosky

P.O. Box 11 • Poplarfield, Manitoba, Canada R0C 2N0
phone/fax: (204) 376-5380

For decades, the Northern Interlake Region of Manitoba has been one of the major flyways for waterfowl. A knowledgeable and hard-working staff of guides, along with updated equipment and decoy spreads, puts the hunter into daily action for the various species of Canada, snow and blue geese. More than a dozen species of ducks are taken every year over both field and water setups.

This is the first agricultural area that birds encounter along the flyway and Big Antler's crews take advantage of birds decoying to setups for the first time. We pride ourselves on quality decoy shooting over field setups in the mornings, and blind hunting over water in the afternoons. If limits are taken during the day, we will provide opportunities for upland birds such as sharptail and ruffed grouse.

"I would rate Big Antler Outfitters as the best I have ever seen, bar none... A+ all the way...nothing but 'topshelf'."
Frank Barber, Sr.

Northern Honker Outfitters

Farrell Flamand and Chester Tuck
Box 46055, 6650 Roblin Blvd. •Winnipeg, Manitoba, Canada R3R 3S3
phone/fax: (204) 255-5101

Northern Honker Outfitters is your key to the most spectacular goose hunting in North America and located in the famous Oak Hammock Marsh, the largest staging area for migrating geese anywhere. This is the heart of goose country. Hundreds of thousands of geese stage here before they continue their journey southward.

Northern Honker Outfitters operators Farrell Flamand and Chester Tuck have a combined 25 years' experience guiding. We have developed a package for the avid goose and duck hunter that takes the "roughing it" out of a Manitoba hunt.

We prefer smaller groups in order to provide a personal touch and the highest quality service. Meals, accommodations and transportation provided.

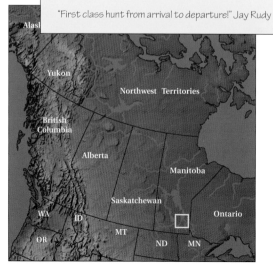

"First class hunt from arrival to departure!" Jay Rudy

Western Guiding Service

Dave and Greg Molloy

Box 191 • Empress, Alberta, Canada T0J 1E0

phone/fax: (403) 565-3775

Western Guiding Service operates from a private lodge on the Alberta-Saskatchewan border. The location, licensing and bonding creates a unique opportunity to hunt Alberta and Saskatchewan for whitefront, Canada, Ross and snow geese on the same day. Also many mallard, pintail, widgeon, teal and canvasback ducks are in the area which we hunt.

Adding upland birds to the mix (sharptail grouse and Hungarian partridge) makes this an exciting hunt. From September 1-30, sandhill cranes are also hunted.

Full-service accommodations, bird cleaning and freezing space included.

"Outstanding knowledge of the area, local ranches, etc." D.C. Priest

Top Rated™ Bird Hunting Photo Album

106

110

Photo Credits

APPENDIX

This is the list of the Bird Hunting Guides, Preserves, Lodges and Outfitters that we contacted during the compilation of our book.

We invited them to participate in our survey by simply sending us their complete client list.

Some replied prizing our idea, but still decided not to participate in our survey. Their main concern was the confidentiality of their client list. We truly respect their position, but we hope to have proven our honest and serious effort. We are sure they will join us in the next edition.

Others participated by sending their client list, but did not quality for publication. In some cases because of a low score, and in other instances because of an insufficient number of questionnaires returned by their clients.

The names of the Outdoor Professionals published in this book who have qualified with an A rating from their past clients are **bolded** in the Appendix.

Danny W. Alberson
Terry Alcorn
Samuel Gary Alexander
Jerry Allred
Michael & Nola Ambur
Jimmy C. Anderson
Scott Anderson
John Asseng
Kevin Banks
Dan Barnes
Allen D. Barnett, Jr.
Wallace D. Barron
Ethel Baze
John K. Beaird
Gerald Bednar
Fred H. Beeman
Mark Bell
William R. Berg
George A. Berger
Michael S. Berry
James R. Bisswanger
Bill Bittmann
Charles A. Black
James E. Black
Thomas O. Black
Jerry L. Bogard
Ray Bohanan
James E. Boney
James C. Bowman
Brock G. Boyes
Roy Brann
Travis K. Brann
Russell O. Breckenridge
Chris S. Brennan
John A. Bridges
Shannon D. Bridges
Frank Brnovak
Jimmy N. Brown
Jon D. Brownlee
Wayne Buchanan
Milburn A. Buckler, III
Billy P. Bullock
Danny L. Bullock
Steven E. Bullock
Terry D. Bullock
Michael Burford
Edwin S. Burlarley
Raymond E. Burns
Rickey J. Burns
Tim Burres
Crystal Burrill
Robert Burris
John True Burson
Gordon Bushby
Jim J. Butler

Frank Cagle
Jim Cahill
Anthony James Calao
Ralph E. Callens
Edward B. Campbell
Lee R. Campbell
Fred Cannetto
William Carl, Jr.
David B. Carle
James Carleton
Dale Carroll
Larry M. Carroll
Pedro Cartwright
Boyd Chambers
Fred D. Chambers
Joe E. Chapa
Bill W. & James Cherry
Edward F. Clagett
Jim Clark
Walter J. Clark
Joe Clay
Charles A. Clayton
Larry L. Cleghorn
Larry E. Clifton
Larry & Timothy S. Clifton
Ron Morse & Bill Cloer
Bonnette Hunting & Fishing Club
Jack M. Coleman
Jason T. Coleman
Dorothy Collie
James Collins
Don Collis
Jim Colwell
Mrs. A.S. Connor
Dave Coppess
David G. Cox
Terry E. Cox
Bert Crabtree
Dewey T. Crawford
R.T. Crawford
R.G. Creswell
Heath Crider
Edwin G. Cuevas
Kent Cullum
Allen Cumings
Britney Curtis
Roland Curtis
Walter Cypert
Robert Daniels
Anthony J. Danna, Jr.
Winifred Darsey
Dean Davis
Mary M. Davis
Joal A. DeFoor
Thomas DeGood

Robert A. DeNardi
Jack Denson
Larry Derrick
Marc Desruisseaux
Marvin R. Dick
Allen Dickson
Danny W. Dickson
Richard A. Dickson
Douglas & Carol Dixon
James E. Dodd
Mike Domin
James T. Dove
E.R. Dubbs
Michael H. Durgan
Jerry M. Dyer
Ann Eason
Edgar D. Edgmon
D. Lynn Eifling
Mike Eilers
Clayton L. Eiling
Bart E. Eldridge
Michael L. Elliott
Rodney A. Elliott
Charles M. Ellis
Charles W. Ellison
Kenneth S. Elrod
Robert C. Ennis
Maynard M. Enos
Dale R. Eubanks
Nolan R. Evans
Dighton Ewan
David & Evie Von Eye
Carl D. Fannon
Roger Fiddler
Mark Files
Georgery Fisher
Roger C. Fisher
Edward J. Fitch
Howard Fitto
Bill W. Fletcher
Adolph Flores
George E. Flournoy, Sr.
Monte R. Ford
Dudley D. Foster
Forrest J. Fowler
James E. Fraize
Gary S. Fredericksen
Paul A. Freitas
Randy C. Gahring
Manuel C. Galea
James C. Gallagher
Neal Galloway
Jim E. Gardoni
Bill Garrison
Richard D. Gaston
John E. George, Jr.

Robert C. Gibson
Conald Gill
Harley D. Gill
Jimmy Gill
Bart Gillespie
Wayne W. Glasgow
James H. Glover
Scott Goetz
Jerry Gore
Robert L. Gover
Randy Grantham
Lance R. Gray
Danny J. Green
Jimmy D. Green
Sonny Gregory
David P. Grein
Mark Gresham
Anthony Guessregen
J.D. Guffin
Ken Burnette Hunting & Fishing Guide
John H. Gunnell
George F. Haigh
Dale Hall
Ronnie H. Hall
Shannen Hall
Lonny Hallenbeck
Trevor C. Hammon
Rick Hampton
Tommy Haralson
Jim Hardwick
Joe L. Harrison
Marcus T. Hartley
Michael Hartley
Ronnie D. Hartsfield
Doug Hartz
Herbert G. Hastings
Paul H. Hawkins, Jr.
Gary M. Haynie
Michael I. Hays
Lowdon Heller
Carolyn S. & Donley G. Helms
Clifford L. Hembree
W. Tilghman Hemsley
Earl Steve Henry
Eric C. Henry
Stanley D. Herring
Eric T. Hess
Scott Higgins
John W. Hill
Johnnie E. Hoda
Chris Hodge
Matt Hodges
Carol G. Hoff
Randy Hoisington
Keith Hoistad

Rick A. Hoistad
Curtis Honeyman
Daniel J. Hooks
Lloyd G. Hoover
David Hopf
Mark Hopson
James A. Howey
Thomas A. Hunt
John K. Hutchison
Sammy Hutton
Garry A. Ives
Larry H. Ives
Tommy O. Ives
John W. Jackson
Mike H. Jacobs
Randall James
Robert C. Janks
Marc Jarrard
William W. Jespersen
Jason Jetton
Kerry S. Johnson
Phil Johnson
Phil Johnson
Dale R. Jones
Stan Jones
Ricky M. Joshlin
Johnny K, Gossage
Kevin S. Kagebein
Kye L. Keffer
Steve Keffer
Michael E. Kelly
Leo R. Kennedy
Mark N. Knight
William R. Knox
Harold L. Kocher
John C. Kostick
Raymond L. Kraft, III
Anthony R. Kure
Ronald L. Ladd
Ronald L. Lagaree
Mark Lathrop
Sue Ellen Leager
Joe LeBlanc
Brandon M. Leder
Emile Ledine, Jr.
Scott M. Leibrock
Jason A. Leiva
Samuel R. Leonard, Jr.
Frank Leverette
Dean Lindley
Frankie M. Lindsey
Kelly Lindsey
Steven P. Lisko
Mayo Livingston, Jr.
Ricky K. Loewer
Wayne A. Loewer
Ronald Longmire
Eddie Longnecker
Arthur J. Longtin
Buddy Looper
Brian Loudermilk
Mark Maier
Roger Martin
Harry C. Mason, Jr.
Wayne Masters
Allen D. Mathews
David G. Matthews
Donnie Mawyer
Arthur Mazzier
Kit (Lee) McCahren
Michael McCain
Kenneth V. McCollum
Roy O. McCollum

Joseph K. McCullough
Michael P. McGuire
Danny McIntyre
Steve Meacham
Wiley Meacham
Michael D. Medford
Danny W. Mello, Jr.
Joe R. Melvin
Creig & Lionel Mercier
John Metzger
Louis Milani, Jr.
Gary K. Miley
Jerry Miley
Greg Miller
Jeffrey Michael Miller
Matthew M. Miller
Ed Miranda, Jr.
Dennis Molock
James Moore
Lloyd K. Moore, Jr.
Terry L. Morris
Mark R. Morrison
Thayn Morton
Scott J. & Oscar Moser
Wayne Moser
Todd B. Mulloy
James D. Murphy
Jimmie L. Murray, Jr.
Steven W. Murray
T.M. Myrick
Gary Nagel
Robert T. Nash
Dirk Neal
Tim Neal
Darryl L. Nesler
Jack O. Nesler
Robert B. Newkirk
Philip A. Niblock
Albert Noble
Craig Novak
Latson B. O'Neal
John B. Ogden
Robert M. Ortiz
Tim Osborn
Plantation Outfitters
Jeffrey C. Pace
Clark D. Padgett
Paul Parnell
Clay Pecvey
Ken Penland
Art Penoli
Mike M. Perry
James Petersen
Charles T. Petty
Perry Pfafenberger
Harry Phelps
Bruce W. Phillips
Tim Phillips
Casey Pickney
George R. Pidgeon, Jr.
Scott Pitlick
Patrick M. Pitt
Big D Plantation
Fox Creek Plantation
Alan T. Poore, Jr.
Shannon Porter
Kevin Post
Danee Sink Shooting
Preserve
Double W W Hunting
Preserve
Jennings Bluff Hunting
Preserve

Sid's Hunting Preserve
Ron Prevette
Gary Price
John F. Price, III
Sorin S. Pricopie
Jeffery S. Qualls
Mike Ragsdale
Dizie Wildlife Safaris at FX Bar
Ranch
Two Rivers Ranch
Patrick M. Reber
John J. Reddman
John T. Reidhar
Ernest Neal Reidhead
Richard, Linda & Rick Easton
Robert L. Richardson
Mitchell R. Riddle
Thomas M. Ridlle
Jimmie V. Rizzo, III
William K. Robertson
Gregory T. Robinson
Jeffrey W. Robinson
Tommy F. Robinson
Dave Rohlman
James Ronquest
Bryan D. Rosenquist
Christopher P. Rothes
Bill Rush
Jerry E. Rushing
Jeffery Lee Ruth
Ronnie Rutherford
Gus Salcido
Alfred D. Sanders
Stephen S. Saranie
Jack C. Scerons
Robert Scheer
David J. Schimmel
Kenneth P. Schrader
Larry Schultz
Steven A. Schultz
William M. Scrobie
James R. Seaboldt
Martin D. Serna
Fin & Feather Guide Service
Paul Shannon
Eddie Earl Shaw, Jr.
Ray Shepherd
Gregory S. Sheppard
John & Mark D. Sheppard
C.B. Shields
Randy Shipp
Gerald M. Shivers, Jr.
Keith A. Shumard
Paul A. Siegel
James Sigman
Don R. Simic
Hayward Simmons, Jr.
Jimmy D. Simpson
Brett H. Sims
James A. Sims
Soren Siren
Gary W. Skinner
Mark T. Slack
Carl S. Smith
Charles E. Smith, Jr.
Jess Smith
Mark Smith
Richard D. Smith
Tom Smith
Paul W. Sons
Vern Soto
Dudley G. Sparks
Timothy Sparks

Jerry Spillers
Steve D. Starks
David Steger
Craig A. Stephenson
Glenna Stevenson
Terry L. Stewart
Billy Stocks
Alger Early Stoneburner, Jr.
Bill S. Stravrianoudakis
Mike Stuair
Daniel M. Stucky
Dennis F. Swope
Joseph G. Taylor, Jr.
Mike Taylor
Howard Thilenius, II
Kevin Thompson
William Thompson
Garen Tiley
Morgan B. Tolley
George F. Tompkins
Charles G. Tounaette
Roy Townsend
C.A. Trammell
Dan G. Travertini
Ralph Travis
Gary C. Treadwel
Eldon R. Trost
Johnny Tseng
Bruce R. Tuley
Chris Turner
H.W. Turner
Roger Turner
Ronnie B. Turner
Steve Turner
Lawrence H. Tyler, Jr.
Douglas G. Underhill
Dave Unger
Charles E. Venus
Gary D. Vierra
Ricky Vinson
Ed Viola
Ben A. Wallis
Robert S. Watkins
Wayne Watson
Steve Weathers
George B. Weaver
Larry D. Wessels
Donny G. White
Elliott B. White
Larry White
Tommy White
J.C. Whitley
Paul A. Whittington
Jonathan L. Wicker
Keith Wilkerson
Roger A. Wilkerson
Wayne Wilkerson
Mike E. Wilkison
Heath Williams
Bobby J. Willie
Dennis H. Wilson
Kenneth Wilson
Roger L. Wilson
Mr. & Mrs. Ernest Wolff, Jr.
Henry R. Wood, III
Steven D. Wood
Morrell J. Woods
Kurtis M. Yeager
George A. Zanone
Allan Van Zant
24 North Outfitters
Phil Chalifour
31 Ranch Joe Kyle Parker

3H Hunting Ranch
4 Mile Hunting Club
4 Mile Ranch Tryon Fields40
Mile Coulee Farm
Albert & Martha Hicks
4C's Guides & Outfitters Chet
Connor
5/S Outfitting & Guide Service
Glenn E. Smith
580 Outfitters Ron Girardin
74 Ranch Hunting Resort
A-W Wilderness Outfitters
Sandy Podsaid
A & P Gun Club
A J Gamebirds
A.J.'s Outdoor Services
Aaron Parker, Sr.
Aces of Angling Chris Tarrant
Adair's Outfitting
Larry D. Adair
Adam Springs Plantation
Donald Durden
Adams Creek Gun Sports
Adirondack Bass & Camping
Mark PeDuzzi
Adobe Lodge Hunting
Camp - Skipper Duncan
Adventure Guide Service
Steve Brockhouse
Adventure Guide Service/O.J.
Sports
O.J. Chartrand, Jr.
Aerial Adventures
Barry & Lana Prall
Agassiz Taxidermy &
Outfitting
Rick Liske
Aggipah River Trips
Bill Bernt
Agimac River Outfitters
Harold St. Cyr
Agnew Lake Lodge Ltd.
Robert & Marlene Kennedy
Agri-Business Supply, Inc.
Howard Holton
Ahmic Lake Resort
Verna & Rob Hibbert
AK Trophy Hunting & Fishing
Mel Gillis
Aksarnerk Adventures
Randy & Donna Lee Bean
Al's Wild Water Adventures
Alvin D. Law
Al Bassett Montana Outfitter
Al Bassett
Al Gadoury's 6X Outfitters
Allan W. Gadoury
Alamichguy Outfitters
The Molins
Alaska Discovery
Ken Leghorn & Susan Warner
Alaskan Wilderness Outfitting
Alberta Native Guide Services
Ken Steinhauer
Alberta Whitetail Connection
Don Tyschuk
Albrecht Dakota Hunt
Norma & John Albrecht
ALC Inovators, Inc.
Aldar Hunting Lodge
Allegheny Outdoors
David L. Heflin
Allen Ranches

ALP Hunting
Adolph & LaVonne
Peterson
Amarillo Online
Ambraw Valley Outdoors
American Hunting Services
American Wildlife, Intl.
Anama Bay Tourist Camp
Alex Letander
Anders Ranch
Marvin & Rod Anders
Anderson's Yellowstone
Angler
George R. Anderson
Anderson Commercial
Andy's Acres Shooting
Preserve
Jack H. Anderson
Angus Conservation &
Hunting
Angus Lake Lodge
Elizabeth & George Tamchina
Antelope Creek Outfitters
Paul Cornwell
Antelope Valley
Antler's Kingfisher Lodge
Doug & Sandra Antler
Antonichuk Outfitters
Willard Antonichuk
Apache Outfitters Andrew
Marshall
Arctic Safaris Barry Taylor
Argosy Adventures
Whitewater Raft Co.
Argyle Lake Lodge
Chuck & Joan Fernley
Ariola Catfish Farm
Arizona Hunt Club
Armstrong Guide Service
Kent Negersmith
Arrow Lake Outfitters
Wayne Ewachewski
Arrowhead Hunt Club
Arrowhead Hunting Club
Arrowhead Lodge
Artemis Outfitting & Guiding
Service Hans Muenchow
Arvid Swanson
Ashambie Outpost Ltd.
Scott & Lynda Marvin
Ashburn Hill Hunting
Preserve
Frank Pidcock, III
Aspen Lodge @ Estes Park
Tim Resch
Aspen Outfitting Co., Ltd.
Jonathan F. Hollinger
Atlantic Adventures
Brian McVicar
Attaway Farms Plantation
Robert Attaway, Jr.
Audiss Hunting Service
Cecil & Mary Ann Audiss
Aurora Pheasant Lodge
Austerlitz Club
Austin's Service
Austin Tide
Autumn Coverts Guided
Hunts
Autumn Flight Game Fields
G.R. Holz
B-Fast Charters
Mike Bartlett

B & B Guide Service
Bruce D. Baker
B & B Guide Service
Jim Swenson
B & B Outfitters
Robert & Barbara Schultz
B & B Pheasantry
Ben & Mike Beckage
B & D Outfitters
Robert D. Frisk
B & K Guide Service
Bill & Kenneth Starks
B & L Hunting
B & R Guide Service
B&T Professional Outfitters
Thomas Barrett
B. Karklin Outfitter & Guide
Service Barry Karklin
Back 40 Wing & Clay, Inc.
Back Bay Outfitters
Tom Cornicelli
Back Country Outfitter &
Charter
Elbert Loomis
Back Woods Quail Club
Back Yard Birds Lodge
Badlands Wildlife Hunting Co.
Grant Paterson
Baier Den Kennels & Hunting
Preserve
Bait-Masters Hunting Camps
Brain E. & Sylvia Hoffart
Baker's Guide Service
Ray Baker
Bakers Crossing Ranch
Mary Hughey
Bald Mountain Outfitters, Inc.
Terry Pollard
Bales Hunts
Keith Bales
Ball Guide Service
Judd Ball
Balm of Gilead Hunt Club
Rudy & Elsie Messaros
Bang Away Gun Club &
Kennels
Banks Lake Rod & Gun Club
Bar B Commercial Hunting
Area
Bar S - Harry Simon
Barker River Trips, Inc.
John A. K. Barker
Barksdale Bobwhite
Plantation
B. Sanders, Jr.
Barnes Hunting Farm
Barr Lake Hunting Club
Barrier Beach Resort
Scott O'Bertos
Barwick's Sportshop
Bert Barwick
Basin Outfitters
Ken E. Wissel
Bass Pheasant Ranch
Jim Bass
Battle River Lodge
Nick Frederick
Bay Prairie Outfitters & Lodge
Bay Store & Resort
Frank & Laura Walsh
BBD Guiding & Outfitting
Dave Moore

Beam's on the Prairie
David J. Beam
Beamer's Landing/Hells
Canyon Tours
Jim & Jill Koch
Bear Camp Outfitting/Great
West Trails
Garry Nemetchek
Bear Creek Guest Ranch
William Beck
Bear Creek Shooting Preserve
Bear Guiding Service
Kim & Roxanne Molyneaux
Bear Mountain Back Trails
Bear Mountain Lodge
Carroll Gerow
Bear Paw Mountain Outfitters
Eric M. Olson
Bear Track, Inc.
Peter & Carey Dube
Bear Valley Outfitters
Chris Switzer
Beardsley Outfitting & Guide
Service
Tim Beardsley
Bearskin Wildlife Reserve
Beartail Bottom Duck Club
Beartooth Ranch & JLX
Outfitters
James E. Langston
Beaufort Outfitting & Guiding
Services Tuktoyaktuk HTC
Beaver Creek
Bob Abernethy
Beaver Creek Lodge
Robert B. Whipple
Beaver Creek Outfitters
Brad J. Leitner
Beaverhead Outfitters
Jack Diamond
Beaverhill Outfitters
Brent Reil
Beavertail Outfitters
Dennis Rehse
Beck's Pheasant Club
Beck's Treks
Robert H. Beck, Jr.
Beckridge Hunting Preserve
Beer Creek Farms
Bell Ranch Outfitting
Bill Meeks
Bell Wildlife Specialties
Daniel D. Bell
Belleplain Farms Shooting
Preserve
Belmont Shooting Preserve
Bennett Farms
Brian Bennett
Benson's Dakota Pheasant
Farm - Robert Bensen
Bequest Guide Service
Bob Sedlacek
Berglund's Outposts
Wayne & Carol Berglund
Betts Kelly Lodge
Keith Betts
Bevy Burst Hunting Preserve
Lynn Gray
Big Antler Outfitters
Big Bar Guest Ranch
Big Bear Paw Outfitters
John Jebsen
Big Bend Ranch

Alex Falk
Big Burns Hunting Lodge
Roger G. Vincent, Jr.
Big Cedar Lodge
Big Creek Shooting Preserve
Steven A. Basl
Big Cypress Guide Service
Jim Curwood
Big Eagle Lodge
The Christisons
Big Foot Outfitters
Dave & Ethel Flannigan
Big Grass Outfitters
Tom & Judy Usunier
Big Horn Mountain Outfitters
Toby Johnson
Big Horn River Lodge
Phil Gonzales
Big Horn River Outfitters
Gael T. Larr
Big K Hunting
George E. Savage
Big Netley Outfitters
George Walker
Big North Lodge
Alex & Pat Rheault
Big Northern Lodge &
Outfitters
John Eisner & Ian McKay
Big Oak Hunting Paradise
Wayne A. Conrady
Big Pine Hunting Club
Big Red Oak Plantation
Arthur G. Estes, III
Big River Hunting Club &
Kennel
Rich & Rose Baumgartner
Big Rock Hunting & Fishing
Lodge - Gus Borkofsky
Big Rock Hunting Preserve
Big Salkehatchie Hunting
Club
Big Sky Flies & Guides
Garry McCutcheon
Big Sky Guide & Outfitters
Tom D. Brogan
Big Sky Sporting Clays
Van Voast Farms
Big Smoky Valley Outfitters
William A. Berg
Big Spring Game Farm
Big Trophy Outfitters
John Hatley
Bigfoot Outfitters
Ronald Johnson
Biggins Hunting Service
Gregg Biggins
Bighorn Country Outfitters
George J. Kelly
Bighorn River Fin & Feathers
James L. Pickens
Bighorn Troutfitters, Inc.
Joseph D. Caton
Bill Clark's Goose Hunting
Bill Kuntz's Oakwood Sporting
Bill Nation's Camp
Billie C. Lewis & Son
Billie C. Lewis
Billingsley Ranch Outfitters
Jack Billingsley
Birch Creek Outfitters
Rick Peverley
Birch Hill Guide Service

Steven Botelho
Birch Point Resort
June & Bob Gibbs
Bird-N-Buck Outfitters
Ronald D. Thompson
Bird Haven
Birds Landing Sporting Clays
Birds of a Feather
Birds of Plenty
Bittern Lake Outfitters
Kevin Rolfe
Black's Hunting & Fishing
Camps
Juanita Black
Black Bear Camp
Vicki & Robert Lowe
Black Bear Lodge
Gilbert Pelletier
Black Bear Outpost Camps
Mary & Walter Fleming
Black Dog Hunting Club
Black Farms
Black Hills Game Ranch
James Forsyth
Black Island Resort
Mike & Barb Sergio
Black Jack Outfitters
Richard D. Hutchison
Black Otter Guide Service
Duane Neal
Black Point Game Bird Club
Black Range Guide &
Outfitting Service Sterling
Carter
Black Rapids Salmon Club
George Curtis
Black Slough Conservation
Club
BlackTop Mountain Ranch
Eldon M. Berry
Blackdog Outfitter, Inc.
John M. Koslowsky
Blackhawk Valley Hunting
Blacklick Shooting Preserve
Blacktail Ranch Sandra
Renner
Blackwater Plantation
Blackwell's Guide Service
Mike & Joyce Blackwell
Blendon Pines
Arvin J. Boersema
Blind Creek Outfitters
Walter & Diane Dmyterko
Blonhaven Hunting Preserve
Bloomfield's Ballantyne Bay
Resort George & Fran
Bloomfield
Blue Goose Hunting Club
Blue Line Club
Blue Mountain Outfitters
Bob Atwood
Blue Ridge Guide Service
Blue River Outfitters
Howard Carlton
Blue Sky Hunting Farms
Terry Newman & Tim Hofer
Bluebank/Cypress Resort
Blueberry Hill Outfitters
Ken & Lorraine Polley
Bo's Hunting Preserve
Danny Williams
Bo's Landing
Boardman's Resort

Boardman Springs Ranch
Bill Weller
Bob Gross
B-C Guide Service
Bob Horowitz Guide Service
Bob Horowitz
Bob Priebe Pheasant
Hunting C.
Boggy Pond Plantation
Boggy Pond Plantation 1-3
Mack W. Dekle, Jr.
Bois De Sioux Game Farm
Boll Weevil Plantation
Boll Weevil Plantation 1-4
Ben Seay
Bolton Guest Ranch Kay
Bolton
Bomesberger Ranch
Russ & Dale Bomesberger
Bonzo's Guide Service
Jeff Brennan
Boss Guiding Services
Bob Byers & Ross
Scheerschmidt
Bostick Plantation
Joe Bostick
Boston Safaris Ltd
Bottlinger Ranch
Milton & Jean Bottlinger
Bountiful Hunting & Fishing
Preserve Bob Davis
Bourbon Brook Hunting
Preserve
Bowes Ranch
Bows & Bullets Pat Bergson
Box Y Hunting Lodge &
Guest Ranch
Ken Clark
Boyett's Resort & Craft Shop
Brad Downey's Angler's Edge
Brad Garrett Guide Service
Brad Garrett
Bradley 3 Ranch
Bill J. Bradley
Bradway's Hunting
Brandenberger 99 Ranch
Raymond Brandenberger
Brannan & Brannan Hunts,
Inc.
Brazos Outfitters
Roger Webb & Joe Slaton
Brazos River Ranch
Ron Prieskorn
Briar Creek Shooting Preserve
Charles R. Barnes, Sr.
Briar Knoll Hunting & Fishing
Briar Knoll Hunting & Fishing
Club
Ron Ziolek
Briarhill Boar Outfitters
Zandra Slater
Bridger Outfitters
David B. Warwood
Bridger Wilderness Outfitters
Brier Oak Hunt Club
Broken Arrow North Ranch
Broken Bar 7
Hunting Safari
Brooks Cottages
Chris & Christine Brooks
Brown's Clearwater West
Lodge/Outposts
Barry Brown

Brown Feather Shooting &
Hunting
Broxton Bridge Plantation
Brunswick Lake Lodge
Marcel Dumais
Bubber Cameron's Shooting
Preserve
Buck"N"Bears Guide Service
Robert Bandy
Buck Mountain Outfitters
Merv Purschke
Buck Run Shooting Preserve
Buck Stop Outfitting
Gary M. Kochan
Buckbrush Outfitters
Rod Hunter
Buckeye Pheasants Hunting
Preserve
Buckhorn Bay Resort
Outfitters
Lee & Sylvia Donison
Buckhorn Ranch Outfitters
Harry T. Workman
Bucksaw Point Resort &
Marina
Gale Nichols
Bud Nelson Outfitters
Bud Nelson
Buffalo Creek Farms, Inc.
Buffalo Lake Outfitters
Brad Steinhoff
Bull Moose Outfitters
Albert & Terri de Lighte
Bull Mountain Outfitters
M.J. Murphy
Bull River Outfitters
Doug Peterson
Bull Run Outfitters
Bud Heckman
Bull Valley Hunt Club
Maxine Wold
Bullock's Gowganda Lake
Camp
Dave & Mary Bullock
Burdick Guide Service
Shaun A. & Walter A., Jr.
Burdick
Burge Plantation
Alexander G. Morehouse
Burnett Game Farm & Hunt
Club
Burnside HTA - Tundra
Camps
Boyd Warner & Sam Kapolak
Burnt Land Brook Ltd.
Leroy G. Scott
Burnt Pine Plantation
David Morris
Burntland Brook Lodge
Joan & Barrie Duffield
Bush's Goose Camp
Bushman's Paradise
Robert John Rath
Busick Quail Farms Hunting
Preserve
Butch's Guide Service
Butch Waggoner
Butler Lodge
Ida Marilyn Lindsey
Buttonwood Game Preserve
C & C Game Birds Hunting
Preserve
C Diamond Ranch

Lee G. Couture
C&L Pheasant Club
Cierce Farms Shooting Preserve
C.J. Crosby Hunting Preserve
C. Jerome Crosby
C.L. Sutton Guided Woodcock Hunts
Ca-Lo Hunting Preserve
Johnnie Prince
Cabin Bluff
C.H. Martin
Caddo Pass Lodge
Pershing & Marcille Hughes
Cahoon Game Birds & Pheasant Club
Call of the Wild
Boyce D."Bud" Rawson, Sr.
Callaway Gardens Hunting Preserve Karen Wingo
Camanche Hills Hunting Preserve
Cameron Outing, Inc.
Cameron Wildlife
Sammie Faulk & Steve German
Camp 5
Camp Bay Shooting Preserve
Camp Conewango
Doug Lynett
Camp La Plage
The Bedards
Camp Manitou
Jerry Kostiuk
Camp Narrows Lodge
Tom Pearson
Camp Raymond
Fred & Barb Roth
Camp Richfield
Tom, Sharon & Charlotte Kmetz
Camp Stewart
Camp Wapiti
Anita & Frank Ramelli
Can- Hunt
Canada Goose Hunting
David McLellan
Canadian Wilderness Outposts
Jordie & Mitzi Turcotte
Cane Mill Plantation
Lewis S. Thompson, III
Canitoba Ooutfitters
Tim Hastings & Dave Malko
Canoose Camps
Thomas Mosher or Faith Sonier
Canterbury Hunting & Fishing
Shawn Collicott
Canvasback Kennel & Hunt Club
Canyon Outfitters, Inc.
George & Lynette Hauptman
Canyon Ranch Gun Club
Cape Lodge Donald E. Davis
Caribou Bird Preserve
Caribou Gun Club Shooting
Carolina Dorrington Hill Hunt Club
Caroline County Shooting Preserve
Carpenter's Clearwater Lodge

& Outfitters
Jim Lorden or Doug Sangster
Carr Farm E. Wayne Carr
Carriere's Camp
Freda & John V. Carriere
Carte Court Motel/Resort
Mary Ann Veach
Carter Shooting Preserve
Caryonah Hunting Lodge
Casey's Hunting Camp
Casino West/LM Ranches
Cast and Blast Outfitters
Curt D. Collins
Castle Creek Outfitters & Guest Ranch
John D. Graham
Cat Track Outfitters
Cal Thornberg
Catahoula Duck Guide Service
Gregory R. Andrus
Catch Montana
John N. Adza
Cats on the Red
Stu & Dianna McKay
Catskill Pheasantry
Cavendish Game Birds
Caverhill Ranch
John T. Fargason
Cedar Breaks Outfitters
John A. Stuver
Cedar Creek Ranch
Cedar Creek Shooting Preserve
Michael J. Hugo
Cedar Grove Camp
Bill, Nancy & Casey Goodhew
Cedar Hill Resort
Jim Stone
Cedar Hill Shooting Preserve
Cedar Knoll Lodge
Cedar Mill Guide Service
John MacDonald
Cedar Ridge Elk Ranch
Willard Swanke
Cedar Ridge Hunting Lodge
Cedar Valley Pheasant Haven
Dorn & Linda Barnes
Cedar Valley Pheasants
Centennial Charter & Launch
George F. Zenk, Jr.
Centennial Outfitters
Mel W. Montgomery
Central Flyway Outfitters
Dean Kersten
Central Flyway Outfitters
John K. Kersten
Central Texas Shooting Preserve
Centre Island Resort
David Ballinger & Laura St. John
Century Lodge
Rich & Kay Tyran
Chama River Outfitters
Bob Ball
Chamberlain Basin Outfitters, Inc. Tony & Tracy Krekeler
Chan Welin's Big Timber Fly Fishing
Channing W. Welin
Charles City Sporting Clays

Charlie's Hunting Club
Chase Farm
Chautauqua Hills Guide Service
Mark D. Jones
Cheff's Guest Ranch
Mick & Karen Cheff
Chemung Shooting Preserve
Cherokee Charters
John Hight
Cherrybend Pheasant Farm
Chesley's Lodge & Resort
Joe Isfjord & Bryan Gafka
Chestnut Hunt
Chickadee Lodge
Vaughan Schriver
Chickasaw Plantation
Michael C. Furney
Chimney Butte Outfitters
Allan T. Thompson
Chisholm Trail Ranch
Mickey Cusack
Chris LaMontagne & Dave VanNext Space Coast Waterfowlers, Inc.
Chriscoe Game Farm
Chuck Davies Guide Service, Inc.
Mark Davies
Churchill River Wilderness Camps
Klaas & Norman Knot
Ciavola Hunting Preserve
Howard Ciavola
Cimarron Junction Land & Cattle Co.
Cimarron Valley Hunting
Cinco de Mayo Ranch/ Sycamore Ranch
Michael Morris
Circle A Guide Service
Richard H. Archer
Circle Bar Guest Ranch
Sarah Hollatz
Circle CE Ranch
Dick & Sally Shaffer
Circle City Hunting Preserve
Circle H H Hunting Preserve
Circle H Ranch
Pete Hegg
Circle J Guiding Service
J.R. Rodella
Circle M Plantation
Clamus Safari
Clark's Creek Outfitters, Inc.
Ronald L. Britt
Clark Goose Camp
Clear Creek Outdoors
Clear Creek Shooting Club
Clear Creek Sports Club
Clear Fork Hunting Preserve
Clear Lake Cottages
Daniel & Deanne Cudmore
Clems Hunting Service
Gerry Tschepen
Climbing Arrow Outfitters
F. & M. Anderson
Clinch Mountain Guide Service
Mike Shaffer
Club & Sport Fishing
Coastal Maine Outfitters
Joe Lucey, Jr.

Cock O' the Walk Farms, Inc.
Chess Obermeier
Cock of the Walk Farms
Jim & Pat Eagle
Cocks Unlimited
Bruce Shaffer
Coffee Creek Ranch
Cokeley Farms
Cold River Land & Cattle Co.
Coley Game Preserve
Colorado Pheasant Association
Colorado Trophy Guides
John & Jim Stehle
Coman's Guide Service
Stan Coman
Combs Outfitting
Tim T. Combs
Come Away Plantation
Jodie M. Gunter
Comp's Guide Service
Rob Comp
Conneaut Creek Club
Connecticut Woods & Water
Capt. Dan Wood
Connelly Hunting Plantation
Connie Farms, Inc.
Warren & Wayne Lapsley
Conook Charters & Hunting Guide Serv.
Gregory Harmych
Contentnea Creek Hunting Preserve
Coody Farms
Rufus W. Coody
Cooke Canyon Hunt Club
Cooper Properties
Bryce & Jason Cooper
Copeau Creek Outfitters
David Osecki
Copenhaver Outfitters, Inc.
Steven D. Copenhaver
Copper Country Outfitters
Steven C. Harvill
Cormorant Lake Lodge
Bob & Gale Extence
Cossatot Outfitters
Cottonwood Outfitters
John A. Wilkinson
Cottonwood Ranch & Wilderness Exped.
E. Agee Smith
Country Boy Outfitters
Country Lane Ventures
Marlene Reimer
County Line Hunt Club
County Line Hunting Preserve
R. Spencer Pryor
Coup Platte Hunting & Fishing
Terry Trosclair
Covey Crossing Shooting Preserve
Ward Brooks
Covey Ridge II
Charles Hazel
Covey Rise Plantation, Inc.
Robin Singletary
Cow Creek Lodge
Cow Creek Outfitters
John R. Fritz
Cow Creek Ranch

Glendon & Pam Shearer
Cowboy Outfitters
Gib Lloyd
Craig's Place - Outfitters
Dorothy & Craig Osborne
Crane Meadow Lodge
Robert G. Butler
Crane Mountain Guide Service
Fred W. Buchanan
Crane Ranch Company
E.J. & Jimmy Crane
Cranfill Shooting Preserve
Don Cranfill
Crawfish River Sportsmen's Club
Crazy Mountain Outfitter & Guide
Phillip Ray Keefer
Creekside Pheasant Club
Crooked Creek Hunt Club
Crooked Creek Lodge/Delta Marsh Canoe
John & Marlene Lavallee
Crouchers Outfitters
Rod & Carl Croucher
Crow's Hollow
Fred Amacher & Danny Roy
Crow Creek Sioux Tribe
Crow Hill Farms, Inc.
Crystal Creek Outfitters Gap Puchi
Cudney's Big Bucks
Joseph E. Cudney
Cummings Valley Kennels & Pheasants
Cur-San's Clays & Kennel, Inc.
Custer Park Pheasant Club
Cygnet Lake Trailer Park
Bill & Sandi Demkier
Cypresss Valley Preserve
DC Outdoor Adventures
Dennis Caracciolo
D & D Pheasant Hunts
Doug Thiry
D & J Enterprises
Donnie Waybill
D & M Hunting Club
D & M Outfitters Kevin H. Deal
Dague's Hunting
Murray L. Dague
Dakota Adventures Outfitters
Terry Strand
Dakota Dream Hunts
Doug & Rich Converse
Dakota Expeditions
Clint & Vicki Smith
Dakota Guide Service
Dakota Hideaway & Hunting
Lynn Haug
Dakota Hills Private Shooting Preserve -Tom Lauing
Dakota Hotspots, Inc.
Marc Bogue
Dakota Hunting Club & Kennels - George Newton
Dakota Hunting Extravaganza
Sheldon & Brenda Schlecht
Dakota Hunting Lodge
George & Chad Legg
Dakota Outfitters Unlimited, Inc.

Larry Brooks
Dakota Pheasant Hunts, Inc.
Larry Braun
Dakota Pheasants
Merlin VanZee
Dakota Prairie Holidays
Sybil & Don
Dakota Ridge
Jim Dailey & Charles Schomaker
Dakota River Outfitters
Dakota Sportsman Pheasant Hunt
Paul Roesler
Dakota Wild Bird Hunts, Inc.
Jack Campbell
Dakotaland Outfitting
Larry Neugebauer
Dan's Outfitting
B. Danny Gudbjartson
Dancing Dogs Ranch & Lodge
Daniel Boone Bullock
Darsana Lodge
Carl & Marg Boychuk
Dartagnan, Inc.
Dave Spaid Guiding
David D. Spaid
Dave Willborn Outfitter
Dave Willborn
David Campbell Guides & Outfitters
Davis Bros. Ranch
Davis Bros.
Davis Farms Preserve
Davis Point Lodge & Outfitting-Dr. Peter Kalden
Davis Ranch
Darrell A. Davis
Dawn to Dusk Hunt Club
De La Garza Outfitters
Dead Horse Creek
Deadwood Outfitters
Tom & Dawn Carter
DeBolt Guiding & Outfitting
Ian & Hugh Alexander
Deer Creek Hunt Club
Paul D. Oselka
Deer Creek Outfitters
Delray Shooting Preserve
Gary Miller
Dennis W. Hammond
Deputy Dan's
Dan Miller
Derringer Outfitters & Guides
David & Susan Derringer
Deschambault Lake Resort
Twylla Newton
Dewey's Hunting Club
Bob Dewey
Diamond Bar Ranch
Diamond D Ranch-Outfitters
Rod Doty
Diamond D Ranch, Inc.
Thomas & Linda Demorest
Diamond Half Ranch
Hilmar Blumberg
Diamond Hitch Outfitters
Chris & Robert McNeill
Diamond J Guest Ranch
Diamond N Outfitters
Brian D. Nelson
Diamond R. Expeditions

Peter Rothing
Dick Lyman Outfitters
Dick P. Lyman
Dick Pennington Guide Service, Ltd.
Alan & Dick Pennington
Discovery River Expeditions, Inc.
Lester Lowe
Dixie Outfitters, Inc.
W. Emmett & Zona Smith
Dixieland Plantation
DL Elk Outfitters, Inc.
Dennis A. LeVeque
DN & 3 Outfitters
Eldon H. Snyder
DNG Enterprise Guide Service
David Garske
Do-Hunt James F. Duling
Doc's Dog Kennel & Hunt Club
Doctorman's Cache Core Hunting Preserve
Dean Doctorman
Dog Lake Outfitters
Milton & Mark Otto
Dogwood Hill Farm
Dogwood Hunting Preserve
Dogwood Plantation Hunting Preserve
Ray P. Lambert, Jr.
Dogwood Valley RV/ Camping Park
Hasan Choudhury
Dolan Creek Hunting, Inc.
Don Alexander
Charles D. Alexander
Don Carvey Outfitting
Donald R. Carvey
Don Le Blanc Hunting Preserve
Don Light Guiding
Don Light
Don Reeves Pheasant Ranch - Don Reeves
Dooley's Hunting
Jack & Joe Dooley
Doom's Guide Service
Chuck Doom
Dorchester Quail, Inc.
Charles Jay Jones
Double "K" Pheasant Hunt
Kevin L. Kline
Double Arrow Hunting Preserve
Double Arrow Outfitters/Rich Ranch - Jack C. Rich
Double C
Gary Covington
Double Cluck Outfitters
Double D Guide Service
Capt. David Demeter, Sr.
Double M Guiding & Outfitting
Mike Romaniuk
Double O Goat Ranch
Double R Outfitting & Guide Service - Glen Nepil
Double W
Ronald P. Webb
Doug's Guiding Service
Doug & Ellie Holler
Doug's Hunting Lodge

Douglas Burbella
Doug's Guide Service
Douglas Fir & Furs
Douglas H. Gauf
Douglas Roberts Outfitter
Douglas A. Roberts
Dove Ranch
Levetta L. & Sandra L. May
Dr. Eyrl's Gunning Service, Inc.
Frank L. Katkauskas
Dr. Steve Mack Native Guide
Drake's Landing
Drake's Landing
Bo Sloan & Don Clark
Driftwood Lodge Harold Schmidt
Drover's Labrador Adventures Alonzo Drover
Dry Lake Hunting Service
Mike Hill
Drybrook Environmental Adventures
Martin C. Giuliano
Duarte Outfitters
Elmer Duarte
Duck's Home
Duck Bay Lodge
Dave & Sheree Swistun
Duck Hole Outfitters
Chuck & Certy Aldison
Duck Mountain Lodge & Outfitters
Les, Diana & Randy Nelson
Ducks & Ducks, Inc.
Duerr Game Farm
Jim Duerr
Duncan Lake Camp
Ed & Faye Barnstaple
Dunlap's Charter Service
Capt. Rick Dunlap
Duppy's Duck Hunting
Charles "Duppy" Dupslaff
Dye Creek Preserve
Dymond Lake Outfitters Ltd.
Doug Webber
E & Z Inc./Whitewater Outfitters
Zeke & Erlene West
Eagle's Nest Sporting Camp
Arnold Drost
Eagle Lake & Katy Prairie Outfitters
Eagle Lake Lodge
Orrie & Paula Colegrove
Eagle Nest Lodge
Keith Kelly
Eagle Outfitters
Gerald W. Good
Eagles' Ridge Ranch
Mike Crouch
Eagles Nest Resort
East End Waterfowling
East Grove Game Farm, Inc.
James Schulte
East Missouri Pro Guide Service
Larry Woodward
East Mountain Shooting Preserve
East Slope Outfitters
James R. Laughery
Eastern Shore Safaris
Eastman Hunting Club, Inc.

Eastslope Outfitters
Anthony John Fowler
Easy Point Hunting & Fishing Preserve
Echo Canyon Outfitters
David-Kathleen Hampton
Ed Miranda's Guide Service
Ed Miranda, Sr.
Edgewater Park Lodge
Tom Thornborrow & Bob Harris
El-J World Class Shooting Preserve
El Venado Richard Herdell
Elephant Lake Lodge
Bill & Sandy Smith
Elk Creek Outfitters
Thomas J. Francis
Elk Ranch Outfitters
David Channon or Roger Whittington
Elk Range Outfitters
William J. Montanye
Elkhom Lodge Jamie L. Wehrman
Elkhorn Game Farm
Mark R. Krause
Elkhorn Hunt Club
Elkhorn Lodge
Elkhorn Outfitters, Inc.
Henry T. Barron
Elko Hunting Preserve
Mell Tolleson & Richard V. Williams
Elliot Acres Hunting Club
Elmer-Nelson Trophy Outfitters -Bill Elmer
Elmer-Nelson Trophy Outfitters
William B. Nelson
Elsing Prairies & Wildlife
Elusive Saskatchewan Whitetail Outfitter Harvey McDonald
Emery's Bighorn Guide Service
Weston E. Emery
Empire Game Farm
Engelhart Ranch Hunting Services
Steven Engelhart
Enodah Wilderness Travel Ltd.
Ragnar & Doreen Wesstrom
Enon Plantation
Epley's Whitewater Adventures- Ted Epley
Erbe's Game Farm
Erie Sun Sports
Capt. Thomas Neurohr
Ernie & Lynn's Birchdale Lodge
Ernie Glover, Inc.
Ernie Glover
Escondido Ranch
Kurt Wiseman
Eshleman-Vogt Ranch
Esper's Cedar Lake Camp
Terry & Kim Schale
Espy Ranch
Jim Espy
Estanaula Hunt Club
Etzkorn's Goose Camp

Terry Etzkorn & Darrel Canode
Evergreen Resort
Garry Morrish
Everhart's Tackle & Sporting Goods
Ken & Kathy Harrison
Executive Guide Service
Tony Allbright & Don Atchison
Exodus Corporation
Richard A. Bradbury, Jr. & Tony Bradbury
Experience Montana
Allen Schallenberger
Extreme Upland Adventures
Guy D. Caster
F & M Ranch Outfitters Floyd Price
F & W Agri-Services, Inc.
Darryl E. Pinkston
Faber Ranch
Leo M. Faber
Fair Valley Ranch Hunting Paradise
Travis & Dianne Hendricks
Fair Winds Gun Club
Richard C. Evans
Fairlee Ranch
Falcon's Ledge Lodge
Altamont Flyfishers
Falcon Beach Riding Stables & Guest Ranch Murray & Marg Imrie
Falkland Farms
Faller's Shooting Preserve
Donald T. Faller
Fallon Creek Outfitters
Monte Berzel
Farley's International Adv.
Bill Farley
Farmland Pheasant Hunters, Inc.
Preston H. Mann
Federal Valley Pheasant Farm
Fence Line Hunt Club
Fin & Fowl Outfitters
Will Beaty
Fin, Fur, Feather
Jim Scribner & Robert Massey
First in the Field Guide Service
First Island Cottages
Roly & Rhea Primeau
Farley's Fishers
Dennis C. Fischer
Fischer's Kennels & Hunt Club
Fish & Fowl Guide Service
Michael Herrman
Fish Wish Sportfishing & Taxidermy Carl Rathje
Fisher County Hunting Coop
Fishing Headquarters
Dick Sharon
Fishing Lake Lodge/Bissett Outfitters
Byron Grapentine
Fishing with Dave
David Christopherson
Five Cedars Ranch
Five Double Bar Farms
Thomas J. Beckman
Five Mile Canyon Sporting Club

Five Star Expeditions, Inc. Ed Beattie
Flat Iron Outfitting
Jerry C. Shively
Flatrock Hunting Preserve
Flint Hills Guide Service
Brian L. Wheeler
Flint Oak
Flint Ridge Shooting Preserve
Flint River Hunting, Inc.
J.M. Tierney
Flo's Fishing Lodge
Florence Lyons
Flotten Lake Resort
Abram & Paula Rempel
Flowing Rivers Guide Service
D.L. Tennant
Flying B Ranch, Inc.
Robert Burlingame & Donald Wilson
Flying H Ranch
John and Amee Barrus
Flying M Hunting Club
Flying M Ranch
Johnnie W. Musgrove
Flying S Outfitting
Duane L. Nollmeyer
Flying W Pheasant Ranch
Flyway Goose Camp Brian Tracy
Flyway Hunting Club
Skip & Tom Frein
Foggy Mountain Guide Service
Wayne Bosowicz
Foggy Ridge Game Bird Farm
Folan Ranch - Bill Folan
Forest Green Shooting Preserve
Forest Lawn Outfitter Brian How
Forest Ridge Hunt Club
Forester Ranches
John & Lance Forester
Fork Peck Outfitting, Inc.
Forrestal Farm Hunting Preserve
Fort McKavett Outfitters
Fort Randall Hunting
J.A. Tonelli
Fort Rickey Game Farm
Fortner Preserve
Robert B. Fortner
Foster's Shooting Preserve
William B. Foster, III
Foster & Foster Ranch
J.L. & M.K. Foster
Foster Farms
Murrell Foster
Foster Ranch Kenels & Outfitters
Jim & Debbie Foster
Four Directions Upland Game Club
Four Men Lodge of the Miramichi
George Vanderbeck
Four Mile Out Camp
Allison R. Corbin
Four Winds Hunting Club
Four Winds Pheasant Club
Fowl Play, Inc.
Barry Sargent

Fowler Farms Shooting Preserve
Carter C. Fowler
Fox Den Guide Service
Dennis M. Coulman
Fox II
Fox Lake Farms
Richard Ramsey Niazy
Fox Lake Lodge
Vickie & Dave Ormerod
Fox Ridge Game Farm
Foxfire Hunting Preserve
Jimmy Vaughan
Foxy Pheasant Hunting Preserve
Foy's Guiding Service Ronnie Foy
Frederick Bateman, Jr.
Oakie Sink Shooting Preserve
Fredonia Lodge
Freehold Lodge Club, Inc.
Frenchman River Hunting Kenny Kitt
Frisco Game Preserve
Fuhrmann Ranch
Walter O. Fuhrmann
Fundy Outfitters
Malcolm Rossiter
Funkrest Hunting Preserve
Don Funk
G & G Pheasant Shoot
G & J Travnicek Hunting Service
Gary & Janice Travnicek
G & S Marina Outfitters
Robert Schulz & Peter Gallo
G B Flyers
Gabilan Valley Sportsman's Club
Gad-About Griz Charter & Guide Service
Capt. Paul Sents
Gafford Ranches
Bill Gafford
Gaines Afton Ranch
Gallatin Riverguides
Steven French
Game Creek Hunting Farms
Game Farm
Game Management
Service - John A. Cox
Game Unlimited Hunting Club
Gander Creek Guide Service
Ronald Dodd
Gander Incorporated
Ivan Armstrong
Gander Pass Outfitters, Inc.
Leon D. Lyon
Gander Pass Outfitters, Inc.
Leon D Lyon
Garcia's Ranch
A.C. Garcia
Garden Plain Hunt Club
Curtis Ebersohl
Garland Kilgore
Gary L. Smith
Turkey Rise Plantation
Gary Webb Guide & Outfitter   Gary Webb
Gaybird Farms
Geese R-Us
Capt. Joe Walleen, Jr.

George Hi Plantation
Georges River Outfitters
Jeff Bellmore
Gibersons Game Bird Farm
Gila Hotsprings Ranch
Becky Campbell
Gila Wilderness Lodge
Robert Rawlins
Gillikin Plantation
Gillionville Plantation
Chip Hall, III
Gin Creek Hunting Preserve
James A. Brown
Glacier Fishing Charters
James P. Landwehr
Gladwin Game Preserve
James P. Colville
Glass Mt. & Housetop
Mike Bruce
Glenn Amiot Guide Service
Global Outfitters
Palmer Harry
Go Fer Broke Gun Club
Gobblers Knob Hunting
Preserve
Donald Deuel
Gold Arrow Camp
Don Moore
Gold Meadows Hunting
Preserve
Golden Bear Outfitters
Walter C. Earl
Golden Blew Acres Shooting
Preserve
Golden Heritage Farms
Golden Leaf Plantation
Golden Prairie Hunting
Service
Golden Prairie Outfitters
Keith Horney, Wayne Luckert,
K. Miller
Golden Ram Sportsman Club
Gooch's Resort
**Good's Bird Hunting/Eagle
Outfitters - Gerry Good**
Good Life Hunting
Gary & Henrietta Stang
Goodnight's Hunting
Preserve
Goodrich Ranch
Goose Bay Camp A. Langford
Goose Blinds
Gladys Dougherty
Goose Busters Guide Service
Johnny Gibson
Goose Busters Guide Service
Jimmy Moss
Goose Creek Hunting
Preserve
Goose Creek Outfitters
John Zwack
Goose Paradise
Harry Prior
Goose Valley Farming &
Outfitters
Goosehaven Guide Service
Floyd Bush
Gordon's Professional
Guide Service
Gordon Matherne
Gosenda Lodge Ltd.
Richard & Evelyn Glazier
Governor's Table Camp

Hugh B. Smith
Grand Slam Outfitters
Mark Condict
Grand Slam Safaris
Roy Lerg
Grand Traverse Farms
Greg G. Wright
Grand Valley Ranch
Grandview Shooting Preserve
Timothy M. Kelley
Granite Creek Guest Ranch
Carl & Nessie Zitlau
Grassy Lake Lodge
Graves Hunting
Gray's Camp
Gray Fox Guide Service
Stan Grose
Great Basin Game Birds
Great Divide Outfitters
Albert F. Lefor
Great Expectations Hunting
Preserve
Jerry & Kitty Russell
Great Northern Outfitters
Ken Mitchell
Great Plains Hunting
Clyde L. Zepp
Great Plains Outfitters
Darryl Giesbrecht
Great Waters Outfitters
Mark A. Lane
Great Waters Outfitting
John Keeble
Great White Holdings, Ltd.
Lloyd McMahon & Glenda
Biensch
Greater Pittsburgh Gun Club
Green Acres Camp
John Higgs
Green Acres Sportsman's
Club, Inc. - Randall Sellek
Green Gap Ranch
Mike Hansen
Green Head Guide
Jack Holland
Green Lake Camp
Charles Campbell
Green Rest Hunting Preserve
Green Wilderness Camp
Linda & Warren Thibodeau
Greenfield Hunting
Preserve
Greenhead Haven
Greenhead Hunting Club
Greenhead Outfitters
Greensboro Regulated
Hunting Preserve
Grey Owl Camps
Greg & Susan Swiatek
Grey River Lodge
Tony Tuck & Dennis Taverner
Greystone Castle Sporting
Club
Griffey Island Duck Club
Griffin Hill Hunting
Preserve
Griffin Plantation Shooting
Preserve
Ted Griffin
Grimm's Woodrock Forest,
Inc.
Elmer Grimm, Jr.
Grizzle's Gamebirds

Grizzly Hackle Outfitters
James Edward Toth
Grogan Hunting Club
George D. Grogan
Grouse Ridge Shooting
Preserve
Wallace E. Rose
Guadalupe Ranch
Gene Smith
Guerra Brothers
A.R. "Felo" Guerra
Guimac Camps
Ralph Orser
Gumbo Acres
Floyd Thorsberry & Terry
Watts
Gunby Shooting Preserve
Harold D. Gunby
Gunners Point Plantation
Gunpowder Game Farm
Guns & Roosters Hunting
Preserve
Gunsmoke Hunting
Gunsmoke Kennels
Gunthunder
H & R Shooting Preserve
H.B. Guide Service
Howard E. Blum
H.J. White Farm
Haddock's Farm Shooting
Preserve
Haddock's Shooting Preserve
Haines Hunting Service
Edward Haines
Hal Valley Outfitters
Lorne Huhtala
Hall's Outfitting & Guide
Service
Keven M. Hall
Hall Outdoors
Rick Hall
Halter Wildlife, Inc.
John Burke
Hampton's
Rick Hampton
Hancock Farm
Douglas L. Hancock
Hanging "J" Ranch
Joyce G. Rehms
Hanson's Bear Creek
Outfitters
Lloyd Hanson
**Hap's Guide Service
Galen (Hap) Munz**
Happy Hollow Vacations
Martin Capps
Happy Ridge Quail Farm &
Preserve
Hardy Bradford Shooting
Preserve
Harer Lodge Don Harer
Harlow Ranch William L.
Harlow
Harold Ives Harold Ives
Harter Plantation
Hartland Hunting Preserve,
Inc.
E.D. Hart
Hastings Island Hunting
Preserve
Hat Creek Plantation 1 & 2
D.R. Jones
Hatt's Ranch

Hawe Hunting Preserve
Hawkeye Hunting Club
Hawkrock Outfitters
Allan Serhan
Hay's Pheasant Hunt, Inc.
Hayes Hunting Club
Haymarsh Hunt Club, Inc.
Leslie F. Gummer
Haynes Feather Farm
Heartland Bird Hunting
Mark M.A. Herbig
Heartland Lodge
Gary Harpole
Heartland Pheasant Acres
Ken Werdel
Heartland Wildlife Ranch
Jay Brasher & Bob Irvine
Hebert Guide Service
Doreen Hebert
Hedgerow Kennel & Hunt
Club
Helfrich River Outfitters
Ken R. Helfrich
Hell Creek Guest Ranch
John E. Trumbo
Hells Canyon Adventures
Bret & Doris Armacost
Helms Canyon Hunt Club
Hemp's Camp & Air Foleyet
Richard & Evelyn Glazier
Henderson's Hunting Camps,
Ltd. Robert & Glenna
Henderson
Henry's Fork Anglers, Inc.
Michael J. Lawson
Henry L. Stewart, Jr.
Herb's Wolf River White water
Rafting
Heritage Outfitters
Ralph D. Holowaty
Herradura Ranch, Inc.
Hett Hollow
John R. Hett
Hextall's Shooting Lodge
J. Hextall
Hi Point Hunting Club
Hi Valley Outfitters, Inc.
Bill Wright, Pres.
Hickman's Gamebird
Hunting
Hickory Grove Hunt Club
Michael Wirth
Hickory Grove Plantation
Collins Knight
Hickory Ridge Shooting
Preserve
Gregory B. Hill
Hidden Haven Shooting
Preserve
Hidden Lake Outfitters
Henry W. Krenka
Hidden Meadow Farm
Hidden Valley Camp-
ground
Hidden Valley Hunting
Club - Bob Anderson
Hide-A-Way Shooting
Preserve
Hide Away Lodge
Chuck & Danny Villeneuve
Hideout Hunting Lodge
Richard R. Anderson
High Adventure River

130

Tours, Inc. -Randy McBride
High Brass Hunting Lodge
Bob & Marie Mushrush
High Brass, Inc.
Tom Koehn
High Country Connection
Dave Lindquist
High Country Connection
Larry C. Trimber
High Country Game Birds
High Country Outfitters,
Inc.- Conrad A. Wygant
High County Connections
Casey Veach
High Desert Ranch, Inc.
Jay Reedy & Jeffrey Widener
High Lonesome Hunts
Mike Schaffeld
High Lonesome Outfitter
& Guides
Thomas W. Bowers
High Lonesome Outfitters
Kerry Sebring
High Mountain Outfitters
Pete Trujillo
High Plains Game Ranch
Randy & Rhonda Vallery
High Plains Outfitters
Mike Bay
High Point Shooting Grounds
High Sierra Outfitters
John Kuenstler
Highland Farm Pheasant
Preserve
Highland Hunt Club
Highland to Island Guide
Servide
James B. McKillip
Hill'n Dale Club
Hill Country Exped. Lois Hill
Hill Country Plantation
Hill Ranch Terry Hill
Hill Top Pheasants
Harley & David Cross
Hillendale Club, Inc.
Hillendale Hunt Club
Hilliard's Pine Island Camp
Butch & Neva Hilliard
Hillje Hunting Haven
Kay & Jud Hillje
Hillside Hunting & Sporting
Clays
Hillsport Wilderness Hunting
Camps
Mark & Karen Stephenson
Hilltop Shooting
Preserve Hillview Hunting
Acres, Inc.
Bob Saunders
Hog-Liver Quail Shooting
Preserve
William H. Hendrix
Hogancamp's Guide
Service
Gregg Hogancamp
Hogancamp's Guide
Service   Paul E.
Hogancamp
Holcomb's Guide Service
Mike Holcomb
Holliday Landing
Joe Blattel
Holly Grove Land Company

David Abramson
Holmes Pheasant Farm
Gregory D. Holmes
Homestead Ranch
Ed F. Arnott
Honey Creek Hunting
Preserve
Honey Lake Ranch
Honker Hunts
James D. Hartline
Hopewell Pheasantry, Inc.
Hopewell Views Hunting
Club
Rickard Wombles
Hopkins Game Farm
Horse Creek Outfitters, Inc.
Jim Thomas & Rick Trusnovec
Horseshoe Bend Sporting
Clays
Horseshoe K Ranch
Dihl Grohs
Houston Clinton Co.
Houston Lake Camp
Ken & Iona Kronk
Howard's Sporting Camps
Glen Howard
Hubbard Creek Outfitters &
Pack Station Larry Allen
Huckleberry Heaven Lodge
Hudson Brothers Fish Farm
Hudspeth River Ranch
Claudia Abbey Ball
Hughes River Expeditions,
Inc.
Jerry Hughes
Hulse Pheasant & Sporting
Clay
Humboldt Hunting Club
Humboldt Outfitters
Mike K. Morrison
Hunter's Haven
Hunter's Hollow
Elwynn L. Collar
Hunter's Rendezvous
John Cole
Hunter's Ridge Hunt Club
David M. Fischer
Hunter's Trail
Carl L. Salling
Hunters Creek Club, Inc.
Charles P. Mann
Hunters Montana
Keith J. Atcheson
Hunters Quest Game Ranch
Ted R. Fitzgerald, Jr.
Hunting Creek Quail &
Pheasant
Hunting Farm Management
Jim & Beth Dwiggins
Hunting Sports Plus
Hunting Unlimited
Larry B. Hanold
Husman Preserve
Donald Husman
I-69 Shooting Preserve
I & R Outfitters
A. H. Knowles
Idaho Afloat Bruce Howard
Idle Grass Shooting
Preserve - JPaul Trulock
Idlewilde Plantation
D. Jack Davis
Indian Archery Outfitters

Indian Creek Guest Ranch
Jon Bower
Indian Hills Farm, Inc.
Hersh & Karen Kendall
Indian Hills Resort
Indian Rock Camps
Indian Springs Ranch
Frank A. Stanush
Indian Trail Outfitters
Bob Cherepak
Ingalls Prairie Wildfowl
Hunts - Jim Ingalls
Interactive Outdoors
Tim Bradley
Intermountain Excursions
Darell Bentz
Isaacson's Pheasant Farm Is-
land Lake Camp
Gord & Ellie Mitchell
Island Plantation
J & B Waterfowl Guide
Service - Jim Thompson, Jr.
J & D Jumbo Outfitters/K. &
C. Outfitting
Jim Hoard & Kathy Hoard
J & E Hunting Club
Earl W. Stone
J & H Game Farm
J & J Guide Service
Jamie & Juanita Byrne
J & L Game Bird Farms
Jackie W. Etheredge
J & P Hunting Lodge
J & S Trophy Hunts
J B Outfitters
Gil & Carol Wammen
J B Ranch Mark Balette
J D Z Game Farm
J. Kenneth Cox Preserve
J. Kenneth Cox
J. Lloyd Woods Game
Leases
J. R.'s Outfitting
John W. Rudyk
J.D.'s Hunting & Fishing
Lodge
Jim Ducharme
J.E.M.P.
J.M.J. Guide Service
J.W. Hunting Preserve
J/L Ranch Outfitter and
Guides Inc.
Linda & Joe Jessup
Jack Island Gun Club
Jackson's Arctic Circle Tours
Wilfred Jackson
Jackson Hole Llamas
Jacobs Ranch
Freddie Copps
Jake's Buck n Rut Hunting
Camp
Jake's Horses, Inc.
Kent "Jake" Grimm
Jake's Rio Grande Outfitting
Service
David J. Powell
Jalmor Sportsmen's Club
James Bay Goose Camp
Charlie Wynne
James Outfitting & Guide
Service
James & Clifford Nabess
James Storey Blackjack

Shooting Preserve
James Valley Hunting
Resort
Harold & Jan Klimisch
Jamestown Plantation
Jayhawk Outfitting
Jed's Landing Guide Service
Monte Hepper
Jeff Pegg & Son Hunting
Jerry Malson Outfitting
Jerry R. Malson
Jess Jones Outfitting
Service - Jess D. Jones
Jeter Brothers Duck
Hunting - Clay Jeter
Jim's Guide Service
Jim Lucowitz
Jim's Guide Service
Jim Williams
Jim B. Cloudt Ranch
Jim B. Cloudt
Jim Borovicka Everglades
Explorers
Jim Kelly Kelly's Outdoors
Jim McBee Outfitter
James L. McBee
Jim Sutton's Waterfowl
Hunting Service
Jim Sutton
Jimm Robinson's Famous
Sports Afield
Dick & Judy Wallin
Jimmy's Quail Hunting
James C. Morris
Joe Rush Guide & Outfitter
Joe Rush
Joey O'Bannon J & R
Outfitters
John B. Wright Farms 1 & 2
John B. Wright, Jr.
John Gill Farm
John Gill
John Haney Flyfishing
Services
John W. Haney
Jon & Gertrude Polcyn
Jonakin Creek Hunt Club
Jones Island Hunt Club
Judith River Ranch
Steve Musick
Juniper Lodge & Cottages
Frank & Eileen MacDonald
K-Bar-C Hunting Preserve
K-D Hunting Acres
K 'n K Hi Lo, Inc.
K & D Outfitting
Kenneth L. Torgerson
K & M Hunting
Mike & Kathye Miller
K & N Outfitting
Wade D. Nixon
K & P Outfitters
S. Van Buskirk & S. Garrett
Kaskattama Safari
Adventures
Charlie Taylor & Christine
Quinlan
Kautzman's Heart River
Ranch-Doug, Marty & Virgil
Kautzman
KB Outfitters
Gerald L. "Bo" Kezar
KCV Outdoors

K. Craig Vaughn
Keeley Lake Lodge
Gary & Gloria Callihoo
Keeting's Sportman
Hunting & Fishing
Gerald A. Keeting
Kelly's Sporting Lodge
Carmon Kelly & Lorne
MacDonald
Kelly Creek Ranch
Charles Domingues
Kennebago Guide Service
Kennebago River Kamps
Kenneth Watson
Kennisis Lake Lodge
Adelheid & Dan Buhl
Kenosew Sipi Outdoor
Adventures
Ken Albert
Kentucky Wonderland
Shooting Preserve
Kentuckyu -Tennessee Quail
Plan
Kern River Tours
Richard Roberts
Kerney Park Shooting
Preserve
Kerosene Creek Outfitters
Alan or Karen Lamy
Kettle Creek Lodge, Ltd.
KG Guides & Outfitters
Ken D. Graber
Kidney Creek Farms &
Preserve
Gary Breski
Kieffer's Pheasant Hunting
Richard & Diana Keiffer
Kincheloe Outfitting
Robert B. Kincheloe
Kincheloe Pheasant Hunting
Preserve
King Buck Safaris
Larry Leschyshyn
King Farms
King Kennels & Shooting
Preserve
Kingbrook Pro Pheasants
Lowell Gilbertson
Kirwan Hunting & Guide
Service
Joe Kirwan
Kitten Creek English Springer
Spaniel
Steven E. Salzman
Kline's Sunup to Sundown
Hunt Club
Kline's Sunup to Sundown
Hunt Club Gerald Kline
Knife River Ranch Vacation
Knights Prairie Hunt Club
Gerry MacKenzie
Knotty Pine Hunting
Preserve
Kocer Upland Hunts
Lawrence Kocer
Koeberlein's Hunting
Preserve
Donald & Debbie
Koeberlein
Kohl's Clearwater Outfitter
Robin J. Kohls
Konechne Pheasant
Hunting

Howard Konechne
Koocanusa Outfitters
E. Neven Zugg
Koocanusa Resort &
Outfitters
Kootenai Angler
David Blackburn
Kootenai High Country
Hunting
David Hayward
Kothmann Ranch
Billy Kothmann
Krause's Goose Camp/So.
Whitlock Resort
Chuck Krause
Krooked River Ranch
Kusstum Tours & Guide
Service
John R. Bilenduke
L & L Lodge
James M. Larsen
L & M Guides & Outfitters
LeRoy Ramsay
L & P Ranch
Linda & Paul Hayes
L & R Bird Ranch
L Diamond E Ranch Outfitters
Dan J. & Retta Ekstrom
L.S. Adventures
Larry M. Surber
La Media Sportman's Lodge
abelle's Birch Point Camp
Dale & Linda Labelle
Labrador Wilderness
Outfitters
Christopher Lethbridge
Lac Qui Parle Hunting Camp
Lac Seul's Scout Lake Resort
The Schreiners
Lac Seul Evergreen Lodge &
Golden Eagle Resort
Gary & Pat Beardsley
LaCotts Hunting Clb
Don LaCotts
LaEsparanza Hunting Service
Samuel M. Fullingim
Lake Ground Hog Fishing
Preserve
Lake Herridge Lodge
Pat & Mike Thomas
Lake Joann Fishing Lakes
Lake Manitoba Narrows
Lodge Ltd.
Lake Manitoba Narrows Ltd.
Lake Oahe/Lake Sharpe
Ryan L. Weekly
Lake Retreat Outfitter &
Charters - Rob Wilson
Lake Shore Hunting &
Lodging
Darrel Lindner
Lakeside Outfitters
Gerry Vermette
Lakeview Pheasantry
Lakewoods Resort on Bull
Shoals Lake
Lamicq Guides &
Outfitters, Inc.
John & Diane Lamicq
Lampe Shooting Preserve
Landmark Lodge, Inc.
Landt Farms Shooting
Preserve

Langhei Hills
Larry's Taxidermy
Larry Propst
LaSada Hunting Service
Scott A.Young
Last Stand Outfitters
August D. Egdorf
Laurel Ranch S.L. Laurel
Laurel Spring Hunt-Fishing
Club
Lawrence's Camps
Bob Lawrence
Lazy E Hunting Grounds
Lazy H Hunting Club
Lazy H Pheasant Farm
Wayne Hanks & Scott
Larson
Lazy J - Mrs. D. Hunter
Lazy J Hunting Service
Lazy J Outfitters, Inc.
Larry A. Jarrett
Lazy M Hunt Club
Lazy U Ranch
Lazy W J Ranch
Le Blanc Rice Creek Hunting
Ledoux's Outfitters
Lawrence Ledoux
Len Jenkins Hunt Club
Len S. Jenkins
Lennyland Outfitters
Mark J. Tierney
Leon Starks
Lepley Creek Ranch
Matthew Halmes
Levee Break Outfitters, Inc.
Tom Eubank
Lewis & Clark Trail Guide
Service
Todd Langeliers
Lexington Hunt Club
LH7 Bandera Ranch
Libby Sporting Camps
Matthew & Ellen Libby
Liberty Hill Plantation
 Franklin Arnold, Jr.
Lick Creek Game Preserve
Jeff Yergler
Lido's Game Farm
Lidos Game Farm
Life of the South
Lil'Toledo Lodge
Ronald L. King
Limestone Hunting Preserve
Limestone Kamp
Ray Hill
Lincoln Creek Hunting Club
Linda-Vue Charters
Capt. Walt Boname
Linehan Outfitting Co.
Timothy Linehan
Lintnicum Ranch
Lad Lintnicum
Lion Creek Outfitters Cecil
Noble
Lissivigeen Game Farm
Little Bald Peak Lodge, Ltd.
Al King
Little Bayou Meto Duck &
Bass Lodge
 Jim Cunningham
Little Bear Lake Resort
Dwayne Giles
Little Bend Expeditions

Rocky Alexander & Tim
Stampe
Little Creek Shooting
Preserve
Lonnie T. Parkerson
Little Daddy's Resort
Little Knife Outfitters
Glendon Swede Nelson
Little Missouri River
Bowhunting Guide
Billy L. Freitag
Little Moran Hunting Club
Little Rhody Egg Farms
Little Rockies Outfitting
David L. Rummel
Little Stoney Camp
Little Wabash Shooting
Preserve
Gary L. Hartke
Live Oak Plantation
R. Gayle Miller
Livingston Waterfowlers
Llano County Chamber of
Commerce
Llewellin's Point Hunting
Preserve
Lloyd V. Johnson, Outfitter &
Guide Lloyd Johnson
Loblolly Landing & Lodge,
Inc.
Lochlomond Camp
Larry & Deb Hadenko
Lochsa River Outfitters
Jacey Nygaard
Lock & Load Hunting Club
Lockhart Guide Service
Edward D. Lockhart
Locopolis Hunting & Fishing
Lodge
Logging Camp Ranch
John Hanson
Lone Butte Guide Service
Lynn DeWhirst
Lone Oak Farm
Lone Pine Pheasant Club
Lone Pine Shooting Preserve
Lone Wolf Guide Service
Mark A. Baumeister
Lonely Lake Outfitting
Ken Spence
Lonesome Dove
H.R. & Brandi Tomlin
Long's Hollow Outfitting
J. Bonner Long
Long-Tail Lodge
Joe & Linda Beving
Long Hollow Vista Ranch
John H. Crow
Long Meadow Cabins
Darren Johnston
Long Meadow Preserve
Long Point Lodge
The Bowens
Longleaf Plantation
George Alexander
Longneck Sportsman Club
Kenny Smith
Longshot Sportsman's
Club
Lonsford Pheasants
Loon Bay Lodge
David Whittingham
Loon Lodge

Michael & Linda Yencha
Lopstick Lodge & Cabins
Lisa Hopping
Lorraine Farms Shooting Preserve
Los Cuernos
Los Mendozas Ranch
Jose A. Mendoza
Lost Arrow Avery Sterling
Lost Coulee Outfitters
Thomas J. Fisher
Lost Quarter Hunting Club
Ann Walton
Lost River Game Farm
Louisburg Shooting Preserve
Lower Brule Wildlife, Fish & Recreation
Lucky Day Outfitter
Ed Skillman
Lucky Feather Game Farm
Harold A. Bennett
Lucky Lake Outfitters
Willard Ylioja
Lund's Landing & Marina
Lynn Lake Area Preserve
Kenneth & Bryan Anderson
Lynx Guide Services
Larry E. Winslow
Lyon's Shooting Preserve
Lyon Guide Service
Bruce W. Lyon
M & E Outfitters
Keith Meckling
M & G Outfitters
Mike W. Smith
M & M Duck and Goose Hunts
Jerry & Bill Maier
M & M Hunting Preserve
M & N Resort
Wayne Chepil
M L Shooting Preserve
Mike Luther
M&M Whooper Hollow Lodge
Martin & Marie Budaker
M. Kuchera's South Dakota Guide Service
Mike Kuchera
M.B.K. Outfitters
Michael B. Krueger
MacFarlane Sporting Camps
Dixon MacFarlane
Mackay Wilderness River Trips, Inc.
Brent Estep
Mad River Boat Trips
Breck O'Neill
Mad River Sportsman's Club
Magnolia Shooting Preserve
Maiden Bay Camp
Joan & Bill Hubbard
Maier Pheasant Farm & Hunting
Main Game Bird Guides
Maine Outdoors
Don Kleiner
Majestic Guide Service
Lloyd Morrison & Don Kobold
Major Ave. Hunt Club
Malarkey Cabin Guiding Service
Ray Dillon

Malinmor Sporting Estate, Inc.
Mallardith Northwest Adventures
Mamozekel Lodge & Cabins - Shirley Mahaney
Manfred Racine's Guiding & Outfitting Svce.
Manfred Racine
Mangas Outfitters
Manitoba Buck Masters
William Friesen & Gary Langan
Manitoba Trophy Outposts
Brett & Judy Geary
Mann Lake Outfitters
Larry K Stoudt
Mantagao Outfitters
Buddy or Marlene Chudy
Maple Island Hunt Club
Mark Young's Hunting Services
Mark E. Young
Markover Game Farm
Marlin Marv's Guiding Ltd.
Marvin Anderson
Marrs' Farms
Gary Marrs
Marsh Hunting Preserve
Windel Marsh
Marshall Quelch Outfitters
Marshall Quelch
Martin's Camp
Bing & Dainne Hoddinott
Martz's Gap View Hunting Preserve Marvin Spiller
Mason's Branch Hunting Preserve
Mason Dixon Hunting Farm
Master Rack Lodge
Jay L. & Lynne Pipkins
Matapeak Ranch
James H. Scott
Matheson Island Lodge Ltd.
Marc Collette
Maurice's Sportsman Outfitters
Maurice or Sandra Thibert
Maurice River Stool Ducks
Dick Henderson
May's Brook Camp
Wilson H. Briggs
McClelland's Guide Service
Jack McClelland
McCollum's Hunting Preserve
McCullom Lake Hunt Club
McDonough Outfitters
Robert McDonough
McFarland & White Ranch
Gilber"Mac"White
Mead's Spruce Island Camp
Suzy Mead; Harv & Janna Sadlovsky
Meadow Brook Game Farm
Meadows Grove Sportsmen
Medary Creek Hunt Club
Tim Jensen
Medhia Shooting Preserve
Medicine Creek Pheasant Ranch, Inc.
Mike Authier

Medicine Lake Outfitters
Tom Heintz
Megabucks Outfitting
David Olson & Darren Cook
Melot's Sportsman Club
Memquisit Lodge Inc.
Jeanne Trivett
Menoken Wildlife Park
Mercer Outfitting
Ken & Pat Auckland
Merck's Shooting Preserve
Walter C. Merck
Meridian Outfitters
Terrence & Robert Truthwaite
Merrimac Farm Hunting Preserve
Merritt's Buckhorn Ranch
Lamont & Shirley Merritt
Merv Mackey's Wilderness Outfitters Mervin Mackey
Michael & Nola Ambur
Michael A. Wespiser
Wild West Hunting Service
Michel Lodge
Wayne & Kathy Berumen
Michigan Sportsman's Hunt Club, Inc.
Lawrence S. Joseph
Mid-America Adventure
Mid-Michigan Rooster Ranch
Daniel F. Stomber
Mid Columbia Outfitters
Mike Jones
Mid Dakota Pheasant Lodge
Joe Hanten
Middle Fork Lodge, Inc.
Mary Ossenkop & Scott Farr
Middle Fork Rapid Transit #1 Greg Edson
Middle Fork River Expeditions, Inc.
Patrick Ridle
Middle Fork River Tours
Kurt Selisch
Middle Fork River Tours, Inc.
Phil B. Crabtree
Middle Fork Wilderness Outfitters, Inc.
Gary Shelton
Middlefork Valley Shooting Sports
Mark Diedrich
Midway Farms, Inc.
Midwest Outfitters
Scott A. Wilkins
Mike Acreman Dixie Wildlife Safaris & Taxidermy
Mike Kuchera's So. Dakota Guide Serv.
Mike Kuchera
Mike Raahauge Shooting Enterprises
Milam Bowhunting
Mike Milam
Mill Creek Hunting Preserve   Jesse W. Exley
Mill Creek Hunting Preserve   Charles W. Penning
Millbrook Hunting Club
Millcreek Hunting Preserve, Inc.
Milligan Brand Outfitters

Lewis E. Pearcy
Mills Shooting Preserve
Millstream Preserve
Mimbres Outfitters
Mark Miller
Mini Sho Sho (Clark's) Goose Camp
Kenny Brandner
Ministikwan Lodge
Dave Werner
Mink Creek Outfitters
Mike Dudar
Minnesota Horse & Hunt Club
Minor Bay Camps Ltd.
Randy Duvell
Miramichi Fish Inn
Miramichi Gray Rapids Lodge, Guy A. Smith
Miramichi Inn Andre Godin
Mississippi Delta Hunts
Steve Prather
Mississippi Mallard Outfitters
Mississippi Outfitters
Missouri River Angler
Peter J. Cardinal
Missouri River Pro Gruides
Russ Backus
Missouri River Pro Guides
John Brakes
Missouri River Ringnecks
Marvin Schlomer
Missouri Riverside, Inc.
Leonard A. Gidlow
Missouri Valley Guide Service
David Hoffman
Missouri Valley Guiding
David Hoffman & Monte Hininger
Mistik Lodge Gary Carriere
Misty Meadows Shooting Preserve
Mitchell Farms Hunt Club
Mark R. Mitchell
Mitchell Hill Shooting Preserve
James W. Ruster
Mitchell Outfitting
Floyd W. Mitchell
Mon Dak Outfitters
Alvin Cordell
Montana Adventures in Angling
James McFadyean
Montana Bird Hunts
Dennis G. Kavanagh
Montana Breaks Outfitting
Donald B. Lynn
Montana Experience Outfitter
Carl A. Mann
Montana Flycast
Dennis Kavanagh
Montana Guide Service
Edwin L. Johnson
Montana High Country Tours,
Russell D. Kipp
Montana Outdoor Adventures, Inc.
Randy J. Cain
Montana Outdoor Expeditions

Robert James Griffith
Montana Ranchers Hunts
Lester M. Morgan
Montana River Outfitters
Craig Madsen
Montana River Ranch
Wagner D. Harmon
Montana Riverbend
Outfitters
Robert J. Zikan, Sr.
Montana Safaris
Rocky J. Heckman
Montana Trout Lodge
David H. Couch
Montana Troutfitters Orvis
Shop
David L. Kumlien
Montana Wilderness
Outfitters
David & Tena Kozub
Monte's Guiding & Mtn.
Outfitters
LaMonte J. Schnur
Montgomery Goose Blinds
Bill & Betty Montgomery
Montpelier Quail Preserve
John F. Hart, III
Monture Face Outfitters
Tom Ide
Monture Outfitters
James L. Anderson
Moore S. Hunting Preserve
John A. Moore
Moorland Sportsman's
Country Club
Moose Creek Ranch
Moose Creek Ranch, Inc.
Kelly Van Orden
Moose River Landing
More or Less Game Ranch
Moree's Sportsman's Preserve
Moreno Valley Outfitters
Robert Reese & Mike Bucks
Morris Game FArm
Mortenson's Private Preserve
Todd Mortenson
Moser's Idaho Adventures
Gary L. Moser
Moser Pheasant Creek
Mosida
Mossy Horns
Eric R. Walter
Mountain Creek Quail Farm
Hunting Pres
Tony Benefield
Mountain Empire Quail
Ranch
Mountain Home Lodge
Warren Shewfelt & Julie Dale
Mountain Man Guide Service
Joe Eggleston & Tim Breen
Mountain Trails Outfitters
A. Lee Bridges
Moyie River Outfitters
Stanley A. Sweet
Mr. Britt's Game Farm
Mr. Walleye Taxidermy &
Outfitter
Robert R. Check
Mt. Blanca Game Bird &
Trout - Bill Binnian
Mud Island Hunting Club
J.L. Bogard

Muddy Creek Sporting
Club
Musselshell Outfitters
Randy D. Higgins
Mustang Outfitters & Big
Game Hounds
James S. Stahl
Muy Grande Outfitters -
Mexico
Myrtlewood Sporting Clays
Robert E. Carson
Myrtlfewood Plantation
Balfour Land Co.
Mystic Saddle Ranch
Jeff & Deb Bitton
Mystic Sea Charters
N-Bar Land & Cattle
Company
Thomas E. Elliott
N Ranch Calvin Jones
Nanuk Goose Camp
John Hickes
Napa Shooting Preserve
Nash Bar Lodge
Lorne & Kathleen Hawkins
Nate Johnson Hunting Club
Naturally Canadian
Travis Imlah
Neal Atkinson Neal's
Wilderness Outfitters, Inc.
Ned Tighe Game Farms
Nepisiguit River Camps
Kenneth Gray
Nerepis Lodge
Reginald & Cecily Fredericks
Nettiebay Lodge
Mark F. Schuler
Nevada Guide Service
James R. Puryear
Nevada Trophy Hunts
Tony Diebold
New Evarts Resorts
Steve Dokken
New London Hunting Club
New West Outfitters
David B. Moore
Newcastle Hunt Club
Newman Wildlife
Management
John Newman
Nickelville Hunting club
Monty Ferrell
Nightingale Shooting
Preserve
Nilo Farms
Nine Partners Pheasant Farm
Nine Sixteen Ranch Guide/
Outfitter Terrell Shelley
NM Professional Big Game
Hunting, Inc.
Mike Chapel
Noble Sporting Adventures
Nobles Ranch
Earl H. Nobles
Nochaway Plantation
John Simms
North Alta Ventures
Dollard & Shelly Dallaire
North American Gamebird
Hunt
North Camps on Rangeley
Lake
North Central Kansas

Guide Service
Brian D. Blackwood
North Country Guide
Service
Rick (Richard) Darling
North Country Guiding
Tim & Tom Mau, Dawn
Helwig
North Country Guiding
Al Morelli
North Country Lodge
North Country Lodge
Dale & Doreen Leutschaft
North Fork Lodge
Dallas Lalim
North Knife Lake Lodge
Stewart & Barbara Webber
North of 49 Guide Service
Jim Hyslop
North of 54 Outfitters
Glen & Kelly Whitbread
North Pike Hunting Club,
Inc. - Donovan Baldwin
North Star Guiding Service,
Inc.
Michael F. Newell
North View Hunting &
Fishing Lodge
Wayne DeLeavey
North Woods Lodge
Wade McVicar
Northern Echo Lodge
Jim or Carol Eberle
Northern Flight Guide
Service - Kyle Blanchfield
Northern High Plains
Outfitters
Edwin R. Anderson
Northern Honker Outfitters
Chester Tuck & Farrell
Flamand
Northern Lights Resort
Hermann & Lise Stroeher
Northern Plains Outfitters
Doug Dreeszenn
Northern Sask Wilderness
Hunts
Keith Heisler
Northern Waterhen
Outfitters - Arnold Nepinak
Northland Outfitter
Jim Kleven
Northwest Hunts
Northwest Voyageurs
Jeff W. Peavey
Northwinds/Pine Grove
Rod & Gail Munford
Northwoods Adventures
Gary D. Strasser
Nubby Pines, Inc
John A. Rau
Nutimik Lodge Janet
Wilson
O'Donnell's Cottages &
Canoeing
Valerie O'Donnell
O'Sullivan's Rainbow
Al & Donna Reid
Oahe Trails
Jeff W. Jurgensen
Oak Hammock Outfitters
Bob Yaworski
Oak Hill Hunting Preserve

Oak Lane Farms
Oak Leaf Game Calls &
Guide Service
Roger A. Sannwald
Oak Mountain Lodge
Clarence LeBlanc
Oak Point Shooting Preserve
Oak Ridge Resort
Oak Ridge Sportsman Club
Oak View Hunting Club
Oakdale Ridge Hunting
Preserve
Oakmount Game Club
Peter C. Reiland
Oakwood Kennel & Garm
Farm
Occoneechee Shotting
Preserve
Ocean City Game Preserve
Oekfenokee Sporting Clays
H.J. Murray
Okimot Lodge
Wayne & Rona Currie
Okobojo Goose Camp
MIke Finley & Lyle Ebert
Old Coppermine Hunting
Preserve
Old Glendevey Ranch, Ltd.
Garth Peterson
Old Slovacek Home Place
Clyde M. Shaver
Old Spicer Farm Shooting
Preserve
Olde Homestead Hunting
Lodge
Paul R. Herrington
Ole Olson's Wild Bird Hunt
Jeffrey D. Olson
ON TARGET Guiding &
Outfitting
Dan Dunn
One Flew Over the
Hedgerow
One That Got Away
Cliff Tinsman
Ontario North Outpost
Barz & Clark
Open V Ranch
Elmo King Jones
Orban's Outfitting
Darrell Orban
Oregon Blacktails Guide
Service
Perry Allen
Oregon Trail Ringnecks
Tom Hawks
Oso Ranch & Lodge
John & Pamela Adamson
Otter Creek Hunting Club
Mike Runge
Otter Creek Outfitters
Ronald & Geraldine Lavoie
Otter Creek Outfitters
Lynn & Lee Nolden
Otter Creek Outfitters
James W. Wilkins
Our Farm
Outdoor Activities
John C. Couser
Outdoor Adventures of
South Dakota Tony Beckler
Outdoor Adventures, Ltd.
Jim Conley

Outdoor Source
John Campbell
Outdoors Unlimited
Glen J. Gulay
Outdoorsman Hunting
Club
Overflow River Outfitters
Gerald Melnychuk
Owl's Nest Lodge Inc.
Ron Parsons
Owl Hollow Plantation
Bruce E. Norton
Oyster Mountain Outfitters,
Inc.
Dan Hefner & Bob Parsons
Ozark Outfitters Hunting
Preserve
P & H Hunting Preserve
P & R Hunting Lodge
Paul & Ruth Taggart
P.D.Q. Hunting Preserve
Pacey Lake Outfitters
John & Audrey Ewasiuk
Packs
Jodie & Tracy Pack
Padden Outfitting
Bryce H. Padden
Paint Rock Valley Hunting
Lodge
Bret & Edley Prince
Paintbrush Trails, Inc.
Wanda Wilcox
Painter Creek Lodge, Inc.
Joe Maxey & Jon Kent
Painter Ranch
Joe & Cindy Painter
Palfrey Lake Lodge
Mrs. Larry G. Day
Palmetto Guide Service
Dave Scott Cox
Panhandle Pheasant &
Chukar Hunting
Panorama Camp
Denis & Ginette Rainville
Panther Tract, Inc.
Howard Brent
Pappy's Fishing Lake
Par Ches Cove
Paradise Adventure
Kurtis A. Nunnenkamp
Paradise Guest Ranch
Jim Anderson
Paradise Lost Hunting
Preserve
Ronnie C. Guthrie
Paradise Shooting Preserve
Donald J. Mackley
Parches Cove Hunting
Preserve
Parkland Outfitters
Georg Voelkel
Partridge Pea Preserve
Glenn Dowling
Partridge Point Hunt Club
Anthony L. Calandra
Pass Creek Outfitters
Lee Sinclair
Passage to Utah
Pathfinder Guide Service
Robert Foshay
Paul's Place Hunting
Preserve - Paul Nelson
Farm

Peace Dale Shooting
Preserve
Peace Garden Outfitting
Gary Canada
Pearson's Hunting
Adventures
Marvin R. Pearson
Pecan Creek/Dutch
Mountain
Gene Hall Reagor
Perrin's Hunting & Fishing
Blake Perrin
Perry Hunts & Adventures
Petan Farms Shooting
Preserve
Peter Meleason
Peter Wiebe Outfitting/Grand
Slam Outfitter
Peter Wiebe & Barbara Wiebe
Pheasant City Hunt Club
Pheasant City Lodge
Pam & Kevin Teveldal
Pheasant Creek
Raymond W. Dienst
Pheasant Creek Hunting
Preserve
Pheasant Creek, Inc.
Pheasant Dreams
Pheasant Flats
Pheasant Flats
Pheasant Haven Farms
Dennis & Jerry Kuhlman
Pheasant Haven Hunting
Acres
Pheasant Hill Farms
Pheasant Hunters Paradise
Pheasant Meadows Gun
Club
Pheasant Recreation, Inc.
Pheasant Ridge at Saratoga
Pheasant Ridge, Inc.
Peter K. Rittenour
Pheasant Run Hunt Club
Bruce A. Chance
Pheasant Run Lodge
Bruce Solberg
Pheasant Valley Hunt Club
Sharon Wilkinson
Pheasant Valley Hunting
Preserve
Pheasant View Farm
Pheasants Galore
Pheasants Galore
Picketwire Pheasant & Quail
Piedmont Guide & Gun
Howard Scheurenbrand
Piedmont Sportsman Club
Pikes Peak Outfitters
Gary Jordan
Pilgrim Ranch
Pin Oak Mallards Lodge
Pine Acres Resort & Outfitters
Rene & Joyce Lavoie
Pine Creek Outfitting Services
Anthony Nepinak
Pine Hill Kennel &
Sportsmen's Club
James S. Rypkema
Pine Hill Plantation
G.J. Kimbrel, III
Pine Island Lodge
Brian Burgess
Pine Knot Hunting

Preserve   Bill Adams
Pine Lake Outfitters
Al Pinder
Pine Lake Plantation
Pine Ridge Lodge &
Wilderness Tours
David & Wayne Holloway
Pine Ridge/Bartlett Creek
Outfitter
Robert M. Labert
Pinefields Plantation
Pineknot Hunting Preserve
Pinetop Plantation
Chuck Lowrey
Pinewood Hunting Club
Wayne DeYoung
Pinewood Lodge
Raquel & Jeff Lincoln
Piney Woods Preserve
Tommy W. Ash
Pintail Point Shooting
Preserve
Pioneer Mountain Outfitters
Tom & Deb Proctor
Pipestone Point Resort
Peter & Shirley Haugen
Pippin Plantation
Plain Dealing Hunting
Preserve
Plantation Hunting Tours
Thomas L. Reynolds
Pleasant Acres
Pleasant Lake Farms
James Alden
Pleasant Valley Hunting
Preserve
Plum Nellie's Mallard Den
Todd Bariola
Polar Bear Camp & Fly-In
Outfitter
Billy Konopelky
Polar Star Lodge
Norah & Ross Finch
Pond's Resort Keith & Linda
Pond
Pond Fort Hunt Club &
Kennels
Pond Hollow Hunting
Preserve
Pond Valley Game Farm
Portuguese Live Pountry Mkt.
Potter Valley Sportsmen's
Club
Powder River Outfitters
Kenneth F. Greslin
Powell Ranch
Jim T. Roche
Pozniak's Lodge
Robert & Cecile Fielding
Prairie Lake Hunt Club
Jack Knobel
Prairie Mountain Outfitters
Doug & Vicky Oliver
Prairie Outfitters
Potter & Westin & Slabik
Prairie Paradise Hunts, Inc.
Dave Neuharth & Verne
Olson
Prairie Shooting Preserve
Prairie Sportsman Guide
Service
Dick Simpson
Prairie Sun Outfitting

Shawn Prestupa
Prairie View Hunting Club
Dennis Jeffrey
Prairie Winds Guide
Service - Thomas D. Slick
Prairie Winds Lodge
Jerry Larsen
Prairie Winds Outfitters
Lyle Hanson
Prairieland Pheasant Farm
Al & Mike Sandvig
Presa Vieja Ranch
Jesus M. Garcia
Pretoria Station Hunting
John Hayes
Pride of the Prairie Hunts
Bradley & Eric L. Nasset
Priebe Pheasant
Bob Priebe
Priest Lake Outdoor
Adventures
Primland Hunting Reserve
Pringle Pheasant Farm &
Hunting
Prior Tract Shooting Preserve
Dan Denton
Profitt's Farm & Ranch
Kenneth Profitt
Prospect Farms Shooting
Preserve
Pulaski Hunting Preserve
Randy Wells
Pungo Acres Hunting Retreat
Quahadi Wildlife Refuge, Inc.
Lorin S. McDowell, III
Quail Country
Davis King
Quail Country, Inc.
Tom H. Newberry
Quail Creek
Chuck May
Quail Hatchery Shooting
Preserve
Quail Haven Hunt Club
Quail Haven Preserve
Eddie Saxon
Quail Haven Shooting
Preserve
Earl Merritt
Quail Lodge
Quail Ridge Plantation 1&2
Pierson S. Morrill
Quail Ridge Preserve
Francis Fountain
Quail Ridge Shooting
Preserve
Quail Run H.
Hugh McBride
Quail Run Hunting Preserve
Quail Valley Hunt Club
Quail Walk
Quailridge Plantation
Quaker Neck Gun Club, Inc.
Quality Adventures, Inc.
Cort, VanAlstyne & Van
Nostrand
QUAPAW Penelope
Gregory
Quemahoning Trap & Field
Club
Quigg Hollow Hunting
Preserve
Quill Gordon Fly Fishers

Gordon S. Rose
Quiver River Outfitters
Paul Baker
R-K Outfitters
Ron Dare & Ken Warkentin
R & J Outfitters
 Robert Parker
R & R Ranch
R & T Gun Club
R & Z Brassell Farm
Robert Brassell
R L Guide Services
Robert E. Landrum
R M F Guide Service
Ronald M. Ford
R&R Outdoors, Inc.
Robert D. Black
R.J. Cain & Company
Outfitters
R.J. Cain
R.O.W./River Odysseys West
Peter Grubb & Betsy Bowen
R.W. Outfitters
Robert W. Wetzel
Rafter S Ranch
John M. Sirman
Rainbow Outfitters
Terry Leochko
Rainbow River Lodge
Chris Goll
Ralph Bellman Golden Eye
Sales, Inc.
Ralph Erickson Hunting
Preserve
Ranch Country Outfitters
Perry McCormick
Ranch Escondido
Eduardo Guajardo
Rancho de Los Jefes
Randee Ranch Randee
Fagan
Randy Petrich Big Game
Hunts
Randy Petrich
Randy Rathie Outfitter
Range Line Hunt Club
Ravenwood Hunting
Preserve
Ray's Camp
Ray Ingold's Shooting
Preserve
Ray Marshall's Guide Service
Reading Reg. Hunting Area,
Real Ranch Living
Terry & Laurie Goehring
Rech Ranch Anna Rech
Red Bank Ale & Quail
Gamebird
Red Bluff Preserve
Red Buck Sporting Camps
Sandra & Thomas Doughty
Red Hills Hunting Preserve
Red Label Guide Service
Scott Olson
Red Mountain Outfitters
Jim Flynn
Red Pine Lodge
Garry & Cathy Litt
Red River Adventures &
Outfitters
Kim Meger
Red River Camps
Red River Outfitters

Lawrence W. Smith
Red Willow Outfitters
Jack Haines
Red Woods Outfitters
Nolan F.Woods
Redbone Farms Hunting
Preserve
T.Floyd Moye
Redd Ranches David Redd
Redd Ranches Guide &
Outfitter
Paul David Redd
Redwillow Outfitting
Larry & Angela Schmitt
**Reecer Creek Gamebird
Ranch - Claude Frable**
Reed's Goose Blinds
E.L. Reed
Rend Lake Conservancy
Dist. - Dennis Sneed
Renegade Gun Club, Inc.
Renshaw Outfitting, Inc.
Jim & Lynda Renshaw
Republic Shooting Preserve
Brian D. Racine
Reputation Guide &
Kennel - Gay Lynn Lang
Reserve Management Co.
Richard Service
Reserve Outfitters &
Guides - Bill Jernigan
Rex T.Yates El Rancho
Hunting Preserve
Rezac Hunting Service
Dwight Rezac
Rhodes Quail Hunting
Preserve
Riber Bottom Adventures
Rice Creek Outfitters Earl
Schenk
Rice Ranch Rosalie Grahmann
Richford Game Club
Richmond Hunting Club
Mike Daniels
Rick Earle Rick Earle Guide
Service
Ridge Country Outfitters
Bill Morton
Ridge Country Outfitters
Dean Randell
Ridge Runner Guide
Mark A. Pirozzoli
Ridge Runner Guide Service
Chad Christopherson
Ridge Runners & River
Runners
William E.Davis,Jr.
Riding Outfitting Service
Ron & Helen Sweetman
Rimrock Guides & Outfitters
Bryan K. Adair
Ringneck Hunting Preserve
Ringneck Ranch Hunting
Preserve
Ringneck Ranch, Inc.
Ringneck Ridge
Ringneck Ridge Sporting
Club
Ringneck Roost
David & Alice Jacobsen
Ringnecks N More
David Wagner

Ringnecks Unlimited
Hunting Lodge
Jon Batteen
Ringnecks Unlimited, Inc.
Steve & Deb Craine
Rio Paisano Ranch Casey
Taub
Rip's Pheasant & Chukar
Farm
Ulysses G. Burch
River's Bend Outfitters
Glenn D. Summers
Rier's Edge Sporting Retreat
River Adventures, Ltd.
Sam Whitten
River Bend Mallards
Dee Denton
River Bend Sportsman's
Resort
Ralph Brendle
River Bend Sportsmans Resort
River Hollow Hunting Club
River Road Outfitters
Herbert Weiss
River View Hunting
Preserve
Riverside Farms
Riverside Lodge Kenneth
Hayes
Riverside Lodge
Ed Matwick
Riverview Lodge
Irene & Pat Blaney
Riverview Plantation
Cader B. Cox, III
Riverwood Game Preserve,
Sam Biswell
Road Creek Ranch
Roanoke Hunting Lands
Robert Chaffiot
Robert Dolatta Outfitters
Robert Dolatta
Robert Dupea Outfitters
Robert L. Dupea
Robert J. Wells Ranch
Robertson's Guiding Service
John Robertson
Robichaud Outfitters
Bernard Robichaud
Robson Outfitters
Dale R. & Janette Robson
Rock Creek Fishing Co.
John Erp
Rock Creek Guest Ranch
Gayle Gibbs
Rock Creek Outfitters
Dean Armbrister
Rock Springs Ranch
Rockfence Station
Rocky Hills Hunting Club
Rocky Lake Cabins
Duane & Glenda Bohlken
Rocky Mountain
Adventures
Dan Shoemaker
Rocky Mountain Roosters
Rocky Mountain
Wilderness Adventures
Rocky Outfitters
Rocky L. Niles
Rocky Point Outfitters
Orvall Kuester
Rocky Ridge Hunting Club

Rodger's Guide Service
Rodger Affeldt
Roduner's Rooster Resort
Steve & Brian Roduner
Roger S. Swanson
Lake Okeechobee Guide
Service
Rogers' Hunting Club, Inc.
Roy & Roxie Rogers
Rogers Country
Rogue River Outfitters
Dennis R. Hughson
Rolling Hills Shooting
Preserve
Curt C. Johnson
Romero Ranch Hunt Club
Rooster Ranch Hunt Club
Robin K. Anthony
Rooster Roost Ranch
Dean V. Strand
Rooster Tales Brad Hutchison
Rooster Valley Pheasants
Rose Hill Plantation
Rosee Plantation, Inc.
Round Barn Hunting Club
Roy Rogers Hunting Club,
Inc.
Royal Hunt Club, Inc.
Royal Outfitters
Tyrone L. Throop
Ruffed Grouse Society
Rugg's Outfitting
Raymond Rugg
Rum River Pheasant Club
Running Buck Hunting Club
Running M Outfitters
Monte McLane
Rush's Lake View Ranch
Keith S. Rush
Russ Willis Outfitting
Richard K. Willis
Rustic Range
Rustic Ridge Hunt Club
Michael A. Shoup
**S + S Hunting Service
Gary & MaryAnn Shaffer**
S F Ranch Game Preserve
S.E. Minerals, Inc.
Vance Custer
Saddle Springs Trophy
Outfitters
Bruce Cole
Safari Iowa Hunting Farms
Safari River Outdoors
Barry Samson
Sage-N-Pine, Outfitters
Paul L. Strasdin
Sage Hill Cly Sports & Game
Sagulla Hunting Ground
Salem Kennels & Shooting
Preserve
Salmon & Magruder
Mountain Outfitters
Don Habel
Salmon River Challenge, Inc.
Patrick L. Marek
Salmon River Experience
Charles C. Boyd
Salmon River Lodge
Janice Balluta
Salt Creek Game Farm &
Hunting
Salt Creek Outfitters

Randy J. Hunn
Samara Hunting Preserve
Harold Ivey
San-Pahgre Outdoor Adven./Outfitting
Stuart D. Chappell
Sand Prairie Farms
Thomas Yucas
Sandhills Adventures
Dalton & Marilyn Rhoades
Sand Prairie Preserve
Sandanona
Sandy Creek Ranch
Steve M. Wheeler
Sandy Pines S
andra K. Hudson
Sandy Point Camp
Bill & Penny Higgins
Santa Anna Hunting Area
Santa Rita Ranch
Ruben Garza
Sarah Lake Outfitters
Mr. Senchuk
Sassafras Farm, Inc.
Saunders Floating
William C. Saunders
Savage Quail Hunting Preserve
Saw-A-Buck
Bill Huntington
Sawtooth Wilderness Outfitters
Darl & Kari Allred
Sawyer Farms Layton Sawyer
Schaefers Guide Service #1
Steven D. Schaefers
Schmidt's Landing
Jim Gregory
Schmidt Hereford Ranch
James K. Schmidt
Schneider's Guide Service
Kenneth LeRoy Schneider
Schrader's Eastern Shore Shooting
Schraders Hunting
Scioto River Hunting Club
Scoffield Ranch Outfitters
George B. Scoffield
Sea Dux Outfitters
Sebago Lake Cottages
Ray & Fran Nelson
Secret Pass Outfitters
Steven R. Wines
Secret Pond Camps & Guide Service
Mark Carver
Selwood Hunting Preserve
Senah Plantation
Randal Martin
Seneca Hunt Club
Larry Higdon
Seneca River Hunting Preserve
Senior Goslings Goose Lodge
Pete Ressler
Serendipity Farms
Sergeant Bobwhite's Hunting   Charles D. McNeal Services, Inc.
Setters Rest Kennels
Michael J. LeMasters
Seven Lakes Lodge
Steve Cobb

Sevogle Salmon Club
Michael French
Sevy Guide Service, Inc.
Robert J. Sevy
Shadow Oaks
John D. & Pauline L. Doty
Shady Grove Kennel
Shady Hollow Hunting Preserve
Shady Lane Hunting Preserve
Dan & Cindy Thompson
Shallow Creek Game Farm
Don Schilling
Shamrock Shooting Preserve
Shane's Game Preserve
Sharpsburg Gun & Tackle
Shattuck Creek Ranch & Outfitters
Andre Molsee
Shattuck Hunting Service
Darrell Shattuck
Shaw Creek Shooting Preserve
Sheaffer's Hunting Preserve
Shepp Ranch Idaho
Virginia Hopfenbeck
Sherburne Shooting Preserve
Sherwood Outfitting
John Sherwood
Sheyenne Valley Lodge
Ted & Orlan Mertz
Shihan Pete Traina Special Protection
Shining Tree Tourist Camp
Bob & Sue Evans
Shiplet Ranch Outfitters
Bob Shiplet
Shirahland Plantation
Tim Shirah
Shogomoc Sporting Camps
Muriel Way
Shoot Fire Sportsman's Farm
Shooters Supply
Shoshone Lodge Outfitters & Guest Ranch
Keith Dahlem
Shot's Hunting Camp
Martin Chatelain, Jr.
Siemers Guide Service
Todd Siemers
Silver Birch Resort & Outfitters
John Friesen
Silver Goose Lodge
John F. Hatley
Silver Lake Farms
Silver Spur Ranch
Tex Tom Winchell
Silverwood Plantation
Jimmy Honea
Simmons Mill Pond, Inc.
Ralph Simmons
Simpson Outfitters, Inc.
Mike W. Simpson
Singletree Hunting Plantation
Sisip (Duck) Outfitting Camp - Robert McKay
SKAT
Skat Shooting Preserve
Skip's Bird Ranch
Edward J. Hirsch
Skunk Hill Guide Service

John Robinson
Sky Harbor Ranch
Eli Kramer
Skyline Hunting Club & Clays
Slator Ranch
Sleepy Hollow Lodge
Larry P. Miller
Slipp Brothers, Ltd.
Ronald & Duane Slipp
Smith's Guide Service
Jeff Smith
Smith Creek Hunt Club
Joseph C. Musu
Smith Game Farm
Smith Pheasant Hunting
Lyle & Dan Smith
Smokin' Gun Hunt Club
Darrin Miller
Smoldering Lake Outfitters
Dave Hentosh
Snake Dancer Excursions
Gregory C. Albouco
Sno-Fun Hunting Preserve
Snow Goose Guiding
Donald Barnes
Snow White Hunting Preserve
Sorenson's S.C. & Preserve
Souris Valley Outfitters
Dale McBurney
South Butte Gun Club
South Carolina Whitetail Deer Hunts
South Dakota Hunting Service
Mike Moody & Bob Waterbury
South Dakota Pheasant Acres
James Monfore
South Dakota Pheasant Hunting
South Dakota Pheasant
Hunts - Will Stone
South Dakota Pheasant Safaris
Darwin Dapper
South Dakota Wildfowl
David Lenth
South Dakta Pheasant Hunting
South Degrey Goose Camp
Kenny & Bryce Manning
South Fork Lodge
South Hills Ranch
Bill & Jolene Watson
South Point Plantation
Thomas Stevenson
South Ridge Sporting Camp
William Prosser
South Shore Lodge
John Procyshyn & Real Trudel
South Side Outfitters
Rudy & Marion Usick
South West Shot Gunners
South Wind Outfitters
Brian D. Haskins
Southeast Game Farms
Howard A. Drew
Southern Forestry Specialists,
Southern Maryland Gun Club

Southern Quail, Inc.
Ralph Berryhill
Southern Ranch Hunting Club
Southern Style Shooting Preserve
Mike Dewey
Southern Trails, Inc.
Randy Harvey
Southpine Shooting Preserve
Southpoint Plantation
Southshore Resort
Southwest Safaris
Southwest Sporting Clays
Spanish Dagger Hunting Resert
Sparkman Farm Hunting Preserve
Spearpoint Outfitters
Gary L. Cleaver
Specializing in Fishing & Hunting Adv.
Tony Pyle
Specialty Adventures
Greg Hublou
Spencer's Fishing & Hunting Lodge
Dell Spencer
Sphinx Mountain Outfitting
Gregory J. Doud
Spillman Creek Lodge
Sporthaven Ltd.
Sporting Chance Shooting
Sportsman's Fishing & Hunting Lodge
D & J Goran
Sportsman's Resort
Sportsman's Ridge
Douglas J. Leitch
Sportsmen's Hill Hunting
Spotted Horse Ranch
Clare Berger
Spring Brook Camps
Eugene O'Neill
Spring Brook Shooting Preserve
Paul C. Fischer
Spring Creek Goose Camp
Tom Corcoran
Spring Creek Guide Service
Paul A. Olson
Spring Creek Guides
Adam Knoepfle
Spring Creek Lodge
W.M. Sheppard
Spring Creek Resort
John Brakss & Rick Ray
Spring Farm
Spring Valley Hunting Preserve
Spring Valley Sportsman
Mark & Patty Finne
Springer Run Hunting Farm
Springrove Shooting Preserve
Spruce Hollow Hunting Farms
Spruce Ridge Outfitters
Ross, Jermey & Dr. Helen Metner
Spruce Shilling Camp
Chris & Verva Gaebel
Spunk River Hunting Club

St. Joe Hunting & Fishing Camp, Inc.
Will & Barbara Judge
Stanley's Goose Camp
Daryl Stanley
Stanley Hunting
Stanley Potts Outfitters
Stan & Joy Potts
Star Valley Lodge & Hunt
Gene & Bonnie Schueth
Starlight Lodge
Patrick Schuler
Starrsville Plantation
Starrsville Plantation
Nathan V. Hendricks, III
State Line Resort
Ken Moser
Steamboat Bait & Tackle
Sam Gilkerson
Steffan Brother's Goose Club
Larry & Dave Steffan
Steve Blake Hunting &
Fishing Guide Steve Blake
Steve Fillinger Outfitters, Inc.
Steve Fillinger
Steve Nolin Steve's Guide Service
Steward Ranch Outfitters
Laverne Gwaltney
Stillwater Gun Club, Inc.
Mark A. Beam
Stillwater Outfitting & Guide
Service Brian Tutvedt
Stinson Farms Hunting Preserve
Stoddard Hunting & Fishing Camp
Clinton Norrad
Stone Ranch
Ms. Sammye Stone
Stone Ridge Ranch
Carl Brugger
Stoney Lane Pheasant Farm
Stoney Ridge Outfitters
Leo MacCumber
Stoneybrook Guide Service
Dan Logan
Story Creek Outfitters
Frank Menegatti
Stovall Ranch
Linda Joy Stovall
Straight to the Limit Guide
Service Tim Boline
Streibig's Game Farm & Shooting
Stukel's Birds & Bucks
Frank, Ray & Cal Stukel
Sugar Creek Hunting & Sporting
Sugar Spring Shooting Preserve, Inc.
Louis J. Dallas
Sugarbear
Suisun Marsh Hunting Preserve
Sullivan Sand & Sage
Sully Flats Social Club
Dave O'Neill
Sulphur Creek Ranch
Tom T. Allegrezza
Sumgoose Club, Inc.
Summer Ridge Shooting Preserve

Summerberry Outfitting Services
Peter & Doug McAree
Summit Lake Game Farm
Sun Canyon Lodge Lee Carlbom
Sun Dog Outfitters
Daniel L. Lahren
Sun Hill Plantation & Kennels
Sun Valley Shooting Preserve
Sundance Hunting Preserve
Sundown Outfitters
Lyle G. Reynolds
Sunset Guest Ranch
Mike C. McCormick
Sunset Lodge
John Gilkerson
Sunset Shangrila Fishing & Hunting Lodge
Donald & Joan Lyons
Superior Outfitters
Walter Kolodka
Sure Shooters
Becky Mel - Eric hristensen
Sure Shot Guide Service Don Nolan
Susquehanna Valley Game Farm
Sussex Shooting Sports
Sutherland & Sutherland
A. J. Sutherland
Sutton's Place
Lyle Sutton
Swanson Hunting Acres, Inc.
Janet Swanson
Sweetcast Angler
Steve Pauli
Sweetwater Pheasant Fields
Duane & Bobby Eschenbaum
Swisher Hunting Robert Swisher
T-M-T Hunting Preserve, Inc.
T & R Guide Service
T & T Hunts Kevin M. Tinkler
T Lazy B Ranch
Robert L. Walker
T.A. Smith
Table Top Hunting Preserve
Tail Feather Guide Service
Tailfeathers
Tailfeathers Game Farm
Tailfeathers Guide Service
Al Soderfelt
Tall Feathers Corpration
Talla Bend Wildlife
Tallawahee Plantation 1-3
J.E. Bangs
Tallmadge Pheasant Farm
Tamarack Farm Hunt Club
Tamarack Game Farm
Tamarack Lodge
William A. McAfee
Tan Lake Outfitters
Jim Knowles
Tangedal Outfitters
Tatnall Camp
Rolly & Linda Lebrun
Tawaw Cabins
Emil & Merrel Berg & K. Wolffe
Ted McLeod's Sunset Country Outfitters Inc.

Ted McLeod & Lana Hurd
Ten Mile Creek Hunting Preserve
Ten Mile Creek Plantation
D. Clyde Bruner
Tent Town Outfitters
M. Mahlberg
Terry's Taxidermy & Guiding
Terry Ledoux
Teton Ridge Guest Ranch
Albert Tilt, III
Tews Ranches
The aTrout Fitter
Harley S. Kennedy
The Big K Guest Ranch
Kathie Williamson
The Break Hunting Preserve
John J. Caldwell
The Cannonball Company
The Covey Connection
The Duck Club
The Fraley Ranch
Tom & Barb Fraley
The Glen
The Hobbie Hut Vince Smith
The Hungry Trout Motor Inn - Jerry Bottcher
The Hunnewell Hunting Club
The Hunt Club/Doering Kennels, Inc.
The Hunt, Inc.
Eugene Warriner
The Hunting Lodge
The Huntsman Hunt Club, James & Nora Tebben
The Inn at El Canelo
The Louisiana Experience at Cypress Point
Todd St. Romain
The Lyons Den
Calvin & Mary Lyons
The New Vickery Lodge
Rick & Fran Hubbs
The Oaks Gun Club
The Old River Lodge
Vicki & Alex Mills
The Outdoorsman
L.C. Harold
The Outpost Lodge
Tom & Jill Olson
The Perfect Place
Alan Tharp
The Preserve
The Ranch at Ucross
The River's Edge
David W. Corcoran
The Sportsman's Shooting Preserve
The Stevensons'
Harold R. Stevenson
The Tackle Shop
Tim Combs
The Takle Shop, Inc.
The Timberdoodle Club
The Uplanders
Wayne Haines
The Village Camps
The Warrington Club
The Washes
Third Coast Outfitters, Inc.
Bobby Hale

Thompson's Angling Adventures
Howard A. Thompson
Thompson's Guiding & Outfitting
Glen Thompson
Thompson Hunting Preserve   Thor's Trophy Outdoor Guide Service
Thor S. Yarabek
Thornhill Shooting Preserve, Inc.
Thousand Islands Waterfowl Specialists Jim Costello
Three Creeks Farm
John M. Simmons
Three Lakes Preserve
Thunder Meadow Shooting Preserve
Thunder Prairie Guide Service
Timothy R. Larson
Thunderbird Game Farm
Thundering Aspens
Greg G. Wright
Thunderstik Lodge/Gage Outdoors Exp.
Nova & Randy Niewenhuis
Tikchik Narrows Lodge, Inc.
Tim's Guide Service
Tim Charron
Timber Creek Ranch
Dick Iverson
Timber Point Camp
Mike & Marlene Johnson
Timber Ridge Hunting Preserve
Timber Ridge Plantation
Lester O. Thompson
Timberdoodle Lodge
Neil & Brenda Smith
Timberline Outfitters
Willis L. Newman
Timberline Outfitters
Derald Wlasichuk
Timberview Lodge, Inc.
Tinker Creek Shooting Preserve
Tinker Kennels Bob Tinker
Tinmouth Hunting Preserve
Rick Fallar
TMT Hunting Preserve, Inc.
TNT Guide Service
Jorgen A. & Tony Nokleberg
TNT Hunting Preserve Rick Taylor
TNT Shooting Grounds
Tobacco Stick Shooting Preserve
Tobique & Serpentine Camps, Donald McAskill
Toby's Trophy Treks
Toby Coleman
Todd Loewen Outfitting
Todd Loewen
Tom's Guide Service
Tom A. Bugni
Tom's Guide Service
Tom McKinven
Tom Loder's Panhandle Outfitters
Tom Loder
Tomanet Ranch
Tom Joseph

Tonapah Lodge & Outfitters   Frank, George & Jean Murnick
Tonneson's Taxidermy & Guide Service
Dave Tonneson
Top Flight Hunting Preserve
Top Flight Outfitters
Jerry Grissom
Top Gun Farms
Top Gun Outfitters
Reg Bousquet
Top Gun Shooting Preserve
George Vuillemot
Top Gun, L.L.C.
David Martin & Dale Shumaker
Top Two Ocean Pass Ranch & Outfitting John Winter
Topaz Sportsman's Club
Torel Wildlife
Trail End Camp & Outfitters
The Hrechkosys
Trail of Tears Sports Resort
Ron & Deb Charles
Trailhead Cabins
Maurice Lavergne & Sandy Vincent
Trails End Outfitters
Rolie Morris
Trails West Outfitters
Roger St. Clair
Trapper Don's Lodge & Outfitting
Don & Lynn McCrea
Trapper Jim's Hunt Club
Jim S. Pruett
Traxler's Hunting Preserve
Treo Ranches, Inc.
Phil & Clinton Carlson
Tri Mountain Outfitters
Andy Celander
Tri R Shooting Preserve
R.G. Swearingin
Triangle C Ranches
Ron Gillett
Triangle X Ranch
Donald Turner
Triple B Outfitters
David Gill
Triple Creek Outfitters
Roy G. Ereaux
Triple H Hunting Service
Marlin & Marilyn Haukaas
Triple H Ranch Hunting
Triple J Hunt Club
Daryl R. Johnson
Triple J Hunt Club of Kansas - John C. Gable
Triple O Outfitters, Inc.
Harlan, D.A. & Barbara Opdahl
Troilus Kennels & Guide Service
Trophies Plus Outfitters
Richard M. Watkins
Troutwest
Thomas J. Laviolette
True North Outfitting Co.
Jim Hudson
Tulloch Farm at Gynnfield

Tumbleweed Lodge
Don Bollweg
Tumm's Pine View Game Farm
Turkey Creek Hunting Preserve
Turkey Hollow "Man"
Johnny Holleman
Turkey Hollow "Man"
Brooks Holleman
Turkey Track Club, Inc.
John Hauer
Turkey Track Ranch
John Hauer
Turkey Trot Acres Hunting Lodge
Peter M. Clare
Turkey Trot Ranch
Turtle Creek Hunting Preserve
Turtle Lake Lodge
Maurice & Jeanette Blais
Turtle Mountain Outfitting
Don & Lynn Smith
Twilight Guiding & Outfitting
Marcel Morin
Twin Buttes Outfitters
Paul Mobley
Twin Lakes Sporting Club
Twin Lakes Taxidermy & Outfitting
David Schneider
Twin Mounds Lodge
Twin Ponds Duck Club, Inc.
Twitchell Bros. Snap Creek Ranch
J. Twitchell
Two Leggins Outfitters
David C. Schaff
Two Spirit Guest Ranch & Retreat
Lee Cryer & Denise Needham
TyTy Hunting Preserve, Inc.
Tygart Timbers
Uhlik Hunting Grounds
Mark G. Uhlik & Murray L. Dague
Ulupalakua Hunting Club
Uncompahgre Guide Service
Larry Lorenz & Clark Adkins
United States Outfitters of Arizona
Van Hale
Upland Bay Hunt Club
Mike Mathews
Upland Hunt Club
Mike McInerney
Upland Hunts
Upland Meadows Hunting
Upland Outfitting Services
Upland Sports of South Hero
Upper-Edge Outfitters
Rick Borysiuk
Upper Delaware Outfitters
Bill Fraser
Upper Missouri Pro Guide Service
Ralph Gravos
Upper Oxbow Adventures
Debbie Norton
Upriver Richard Beedy
V-6 Hunting Preserve Corp.   Jack & Joyce

Volk
V6 Hunting Preserve & Guides
Valhalla-Bijou, Inc.
Valhalla Hunt Club
Valley View Hunting
Valley View Ranch
Richard Gondeiro
Valley West Trap, Skeet & Sporting Clays Daniel Stock
Veale Pheasant Club
Venwood Lake Hunting & Fishing
Verdigris Valley Outfitters
Douglas C. Arnold
Verdigris Valley Outfitters
Michael D. Collins
Vermont Wildfowl Guide Service
Thomas Venezia
Vern's Guide Service
Vern & Bonita
Viking Lodge Ted Smith
Viking Valley Hunt Club
Volz Ranch Encinal
James Volz
Von Eye Ranch
Foster & Elva Von Eye
Voncannon's Shooting Preserve
W.C.Flyers
W.S. Sherrill Waterfowl Hunting
Waialua Hunt Club
Waldroup Road Hunting Preserve
James Garrett
Walker Guide Service/Carl's Bait Shop
Ron Walker
Wallace Guides & Outfitters
Bill & Fred Wallace
Wallace McLaughlin Outfitting
Wallace McLaughlin
Wally York & Son, Inc.
W. Travis York
Walnut Ridge Hunting Preserve
Walnut Run Shooting Preserve
Walser's McGregor Bay Camp
Mary & Gary Walser
Walt's Guiding & Outfitting
Walter & Betty Mallery
Wapiti River Guides
Gary Lane
Warne Ranches
Cody Warne
Warriors Mark Shooting Preserve - Eric Gilliland
Washow Bay Lodge
Ron Chekosky
Waterfowl Flyway, Inc.
Waterfowl Specialties, Inc.
Waterhen Band Outfitting Chief Harvey
Waterhen Lake Resort Skownan Black Bear Ruth & Thomas Pfister
Waterhen River Lodge
Clarence & Della Popowich
Wauklehegan Outfitter

Ronald J. Painter
Wayne Hill Outfitting
Wayne Hill
Wayne Johnson Deer Run
Wildlife Hunt Club
Webb's Camp
Webb Shooting Preserve
Wesley L. Webb
Well's Shooting Preserve
Dale Wells
Wells Brother Quail Hunting - Steven P. Wells
Welovet Lodge
Shawn Bowes
Wendt's Pheasants
Atlas & Dave Wendt
West Creek Gunning Club
West Creek Shooting Preserve
West Fork Outfitters
Ronald M. Corr
West Fork Outfitters
G. Eugene Story
West River Adventures
Chris Studer
West River Guide Service
Ray Pitts
West River Outfitters
Ken Dooley & Robert Sperk. Jr.
West Valley Sportmen Club
Western Cross Outfitters
Kym L. Taylor
Western Guiding Services
Dave & Greg Molloy
Western Rivers
Fred J. Tedesco
Western Wildlife Adventure
Westervelt Hunting Lodge
Westwood Lodge
Tim & Emilie Lies
Whale Back Farms Shooting Preserve
Wheeler's Hunting
Dallas & Lois Wheeler
Wheeler Station Hunting Preserve
Whetstone Creek Lodge
Gerald & Marg Hallihan
Whiskey River Guide Service
Vicky
Whisky River Hunt Club #1 & #3
Michael A. Damman
Whispering Emeral Ridge Game Farm
Whispering Pines Hideaway
White Birch Guide Service
Capt. Paul R. Bois
White Birch Lodge
Bob Walsh
White Buffalo Ranch Retreat
White Cloud Outfitters
Mike Scott & Louise Stark
White Game Farm
White Oak Farm
White Oak Plantation
White Oak Reserve
George R. Metcalf
White River Lodge
Udell & Betty Schroeder
White Swan Lake Resort
Gerry Wenschlag

White Swan Sports
Mike Hazuk
White Tail Ranch Outfitters
Jack E. Hooker
White Water Fishing Trips
Carl R. (Skip) Zapffe
White Whale Outfitting
Whiteface Guide Service
G. L. Scott
Whiteshell Lake Resort
Liberty & David DesRoches-Dueck
Whiteshell Outfitters
Mike & Deb Adey
Whitetail Enterprises
Whitetail Outfitters
Darlene & Justin Giasson
WILCO Joel B. Williams
Wild Acres Hunting Club
Wild Country Outfitters, Inc.
Jerry E. Strong
Wild Flush, Inc.
]Mike & Terry Frederick
Wild Goose Chase
David L. Engel
Wild Horse Creek Ranch
William R. Shields & Rick Hankins
Wild Redheads Archery Turkey Hunts
Jason Lambley
Wild Ridge Planation 1-2
R.C. Balfour, III
Wild Thing Outfitters
Tim Fehr
Wild Wings
Rick & Jeff Johnson
Wild Wings Expeditions
Wild Wings Game Farm
James W. Avery
Wild Wings Outfitters
R. Button, R. Ross & B. Carter
Wild Wings Sporting Club
Wilderness Adventures
Joe Lombardi
Wilderness Lodge
Wilderness Lodge
Judy & Eric Wismer
Wilderness Lodge & Skyline Outfit, Inc.
Greg Deimler
Wilderness Lodge & Skyline Outfitters Cameron E. Lee
Wilderness Outfitters
Arnold D. Elser
Wilderness Outfitters
Scott, Shelda, Justin & Jarrod Farr
Wilderness River Outfitters
Bruce Greene
Wilderness Sporting Clays
Wilderness Unlimited
Wildlife Action Resource
Wildlife Adventures, Inc.
Jack E. Wemple
Wildlife Game Birds
Wildlife Inc.
Wildlife Place #1, #2 & #3
Richard G. Johnson
Wildlife Rehabilitation League
Wildlife Service
Terry Fincher

Wildlife, Inc.
Wildwind Outfitters
Brian Schofield
Wildwings Guide Service
Charles E. "Charlie" Vyles
Wildwood Hunt Club
Wildwood Hunting & Sporting
Williams Guide Service
Don A. Williams
Willimans Wildlife Lodge & Guiding
Willow Creek Wildlife, Inc.
Bob & Steve Stoeser
Willow Lake Sportsmen's Club
Woodrow R.Thompson
Willow Run Hunting Preserve
Wilson's Sporting Camps, Ltd. - Keith Wilson
Wilson Ranch
Wind Dancer Guide Service
Larry L. Wright
Windmill Pheasant Farm
Windsock Lodge/Hastings Bros. Outfitters
Tim & Donna Hastings
Windwood Farm
Winy Hill Shooting Preserve
Windy Ridge Game Farm & Kennel
Winegar Farms
Ralph & Judy Winegar
Wing & Shot Hunting Preserve
Wigs - St. Albans Properties
Wings of Adventure
Jeff Conners
Wingshooter Guiding Service
Wingshooters Lodge
Wingshot Bird Farm
Alan D. Pane
Wingtip Game Ranch & Kennel
Wintergreen Hunting Preserve
Wintering Creek Hunting Lodge
Lynn R. Kongslie
Winterset Hunt Club & Lodge
Wise Olde Hunting Preserve   Jean Wise, Jr.
Witte Ranch Patrick J. Witte
Wolf Creek Lodge
W.W. Kasulka
Wolf Creek Outfitters
Jeffrey D. Berkenmeier
Wolf Creek Outfitters, LLC
Jason Ward
Wolf Creek Shooting Preserve
Wolf Lake Wilderness Experience
Doug Schindler
Wolf River Game Farm
Wolf River Outfitter
Jim Aller, Tony French & Tom Johansen
Wood's Gamebird Farm

Woodhouse Camp
The Woodhouses
Woodland Farms/Briar Creek
Woodland Pheasant Club
Woods & Meadows Game Farm
Woodstock Hunt Club, Inc.
Wooster Duck & Pheasant Hunting Pres.
World Class Shooting Preserve
James R. Moore
Worldwide Outdoor Adventures
Randy Beck
Wounded Knee
Dick & Judy Wells
WR Hunt Club
Wrestle Creek Game Club
Wright Cottages
WW Outfitters
William A. White
Wycamp Lake Club, Inc.
Dirk K. Shorter
Wylie Hill Farm
Wynfield Plantation
Larry L. Ruis
Yaak River Outfitters
Patrick "Clint" Mills
Yadkin Point Hunt & Sporting Club
Yellowater Outfitters
Roy G. Olsen
Yellowstone Outfitters
Lynn & Marcene Madsen
Yellowstone River Hunting
Scott A. Cornell
Young's Fishing Service, Inc.
Jack LaFond & Bill Young
Young Lake Lodge
Steve & Debbie Vincent
Z Bar J Outfitters
Mark Story
Zoss Family Shooting Preserve
Adolf & Dotty Zoss

Picked-By-You Guides® Questionnaires

Picked-By-You Questionnaire
Top Guided Turkey Hunting

Name of your Field Guide:_____
(Person that guided you in the field)

Date of Trip_____Location_____ Day Hunt ☐   Overnight ☐

Species: Eastern ☐   Rio Grande ☐   Florida ☐   Merriam's ☐   Gould's ☐   Other_____

Outstanding   Excellent   Good   Acceptable   Poor/Inferior   Unacceptable

1. How helpful was the Outfitter (Guide or Lodge) with travel arrangements, hunting regulations, permits etc.?..   ☐ ☐ ☐ ☐ ☐ ☐

2. How well did the Outfitter (Guide or Lodge) provide important details that better prepared you for your hunting trip (clothing, equipment, information on the species, list of "take along", etc.)?...............................   ☐ ☐ ☐ ☐ ☐ ☐

3. How would you rate the Outfitter's (Guide or Lodge) office skills in handling deposits, charges, reservations, returning calls before and after your trip?...   ☐ ☐ ☐ ☐ ☐ ☐

4. How would you rate the accommodations (tent, cabin, lodge, etc.)?...........   ☐ ☐ ☐ ☐ ☐ ☐

5. How would you rate the equipment provided by the Outfitter (Guide or Lodge) during your hunt (atv, pick-up, blinds, etc.)?...............................   ☐ ☐ ☐ ☐ ☐ ☐

6. How would you rate the cooking (quantity, quality and cleanliness of the service)?..   ☐ ☐ ☐ ☐ ☐ ☐

7. How would you rate your Guide's Attitude — Politeness — Disposition?.....   ☐ ☐ ☐ ☐ ☐ ☐

8. How would you rate your Guide's knowledge of the area?............................   ☐ ☐ ☐ ☐ ☐ ☐

9. How would you rate your Guide's knowledge of the birds (feeding cycle, habits, etc.)?...   ☐ ☐ ☐ ☐ ☐ ☐

10. How were your birds prepared for trophy mounting and/or for the trip home?..   ☐ ☐ ☐ ☐ ☐ ☐

142

	Outstanding	Excellent	Good	Acceptable	Poor/Inferior	Unacceptable
11. How would you rate the skills and the attitude of the Staff overall?............	☐	☐	☐	☐	☐	☐
12. How would you rate your Guide's calling technique?.....................................	☐	☐	☐	☐	☐	☐
13. How would you rate the quality of the blinds, if applicable?........................	☐	☐	☐	☐	☐	☐
14. How would you rate the quantity of the turkeys?..	☐	☐	☐	☐	☐	☐
15. How would you rate the overall quality of your field experience?................	☐	☐	☐	☐	☐	☐

	Good	Fair	Poor
16. How would you describe the weather conditions?..	☐	☐	☐

17. Did the Outdoor Professional accurately represent the overall quality of your experience (quality of area, birds, accommodations, etc.)?................. ☐ Yes ☐ No

18. Did you provide the Outfitter (Guide or Lodge) with truthful statements regarding your personal needs, your skills and your expectations?.............. ☐ Yes ☐ No

19. Would you use this Outdoor Professional/Business again?............................ ☐ Yes ☐ No

20. Would you recommend this Outdoor Professional/Business to others?..... ☐ Yes ☐ No

Comments: _____
_____
_____
_____
_____
_____
_____
_____
_____
_____
_____
_____
_____
_____
_____
_____
_____

Will you permit Picked-By-You to use your name and comments in our book(s)? ☐ Yes ☐ No

Signature_____

Picked-By-You Questionnaire
Top Guided Upland Bird Hunting

Name of your Field Guide:_____
(Person that guided you in the field)

Date of Hunt_____Location_____

Fully Guided Trip ☐   Day Hunt ☐   Overnight Hunt ☐

(Harvested or Observed)

	OUTSTANDING	EXCELLENT	GOOD	ACCEPTABLE	POOR/INFERIOR	UNACCEPTABLE
1. How helpful was the Outfitter (Guide or Lodge) with travel arrangements, hunting regulations, permits etc.?	☐	☐	☐	☐	☐	☐
2. How well did the Outfitter (Guide or Lodge) provide important details that better prepared you for your hunting trip (clothing, equipment, information on the birds, list of "take along", etc.)?	☐	☐	☐	☐	☐	☐
3. How would you rate the Outfitter's (Guide or Lodge) office skills in handling deposits, charges, reservations, returning calls before and after your trip?	☐	☐	☐	☐	☐	☐
4. How would you rate the accommodations (tent, cabin, lodge, etc.)?	☐	☐	☐	☐	☐	☐
5. How would you rate the equipment provided by the Outfitter (Guide or Lodge) for your dog and/or the quality of their dogs, if, instead, you used theirs?	☐	☐	☐	☐	☐	☐
6. How would you rate the cooking (quantity, quality and cleanliness of the service)?	☐	☐	☐	☐	☐	☐
7. How would you rate your Guide's Attitude — Politeness — Disposition?	☐	☐	☐	☐	☐	☐
8. How would you rate your Guide's knowledge of the area?	☐	☐	☐	☐	☐	☐
9. How would you rate your Guide's knowledge of the birds (feeding cycle, habits, etc.)?	☐	☐	☐	☐	☐	☐
10. How were your birds prepared for trophy mounting or cleaned for the trip home?	☐	☐	☐	☐	☐	☐

144

	Outstanding	Excellent	Good	Acceptable	Poor/Inferior	Unacceptable

11. How would you rate the skills and the attitude of the Staff overall?............. ☐ ☐ ☐ ☐ ☐ ☐

12. How would you rate the quality of the hunting grounds, appropriate coverage for birds, not crowded by other hunters, etc.?................................ ☐ ☐ ☐ ☐ ☐ ☐

13. How would you rate the quality of the birds?... ☐ ☐ ☐ ☐ ☐ ☐

14. How would you rate the quantity of the birds?... ☐ ☐ ☐ ☐ ☐ ☐

15. How would you rate the overall quality of your field experience?................ ☐ ☐ ☐ ☐ ☐ ☐

	Good	Fair	Poor

16. How would you describe the weather conditions?... ☐ ☐ ☐

17. Did the Outfitter accurately represent the overall quality of your experience (quality of area, birds, accommodations, etc.)?........................... ☐ Yes ☐ No

18. Did you provide the Outfitter (Guide or Lodge) with truthful statements regarding your personal needs, your skills and your expectations?.............. ☐ Yes ☐ No

19. Would you use this Outdoor Professional/Business again?........................... ☐ Yes ☐ No

20. Would you recommend this Outdoor Professional/Business to others?..... ☐ Yes ☐ No

Comments: _____

_____
_____
_____
_____
_____
_____
_____
_____
_____
_____
_____
_____
_____
_____
_____
_____
_____
_____

Will you permit Picked-By-You to use your name and comments in our book(s)? ☐ Yes ☐ No

Signature_____

Picked-By-You Questionnaire
Top Guided Waterfowl

Name of your Field Guide:_____
(Person that guided you in the field)

Date of Hunt_____Location_____

Fully Guided Trip ☐   Day Hunt ☐   Overnight Hunt ☐

Technique used: Permanent blinds ☐   Temporary blinds ☐   Bird flushing ☐   Other_____

(Harvested or Observed)

		OUTSTANDING	EXCELLENT	GOOD	ACCEPTABLE	POOR/INFERIOR	UNACCEPTABLE
1.	How helpful was the Outfitter (Guide or Lodge) with travel arrangements, hunting regulations, permits etc.?	☐	☐	☐	☐	☐	☐
2.	How well did the Outfitter (Guide or Lodge) provide important details that better prepared you for your hunting trip (clothing, equipment, information on the species and the water, list of "take along", etc.)?	☐	☐	☐	☐	☐	☐
3.	How would you rate the Outfitter's (Guide or Lodge) office skills in handling deposits, charges, reservations, returning calls before and after your trip?	☐	☐	☐	☐	☐	☐
4.	How would you rate the accommodations (tent, cabin, lodge, etc.)?	☐	☐	☐	☐	☐	☐
5.	How would you rate the facilities provided by the Outfitter (Guide or Lodge) for your dog and/or the quality of their dogs, if, instead, you used theirs?	☐	☐	☐	☐	☐	☐
6.	How would you rate the cooking (quantity, quality and cleanliness of the service)?	☐	☐	☐	☐	☐	☐
7.	How would you rate your Guide's Attitude — Politeness — Disposition?	☐	☐	☐	☐	☐	☐
8.	How would you rate your Guide's knowledge of the area?	☐	☐	☐	☐	☐	☐
9.	How would you rate your Guide's knowledge of the birds (feeding cycle, habits, etc.)?	☐	☐	☐	☐	☐	☐
10.	How were your birds prepared for trophy mounting or cleaned for the trip home?	☐	☐	☐	☐	☐	☐

	Outstanding	Excellent	Good	Acceptable	Poor/Inferior	Unacceptable
11. How would you rate the skills and the attitude of the Staff overall?............	☐	☐	☐	☐	☐	☐
12. How would you rate the quality of the area (good migratory route, appropriate feeding grounds, etc.)?...	☐	☐	☐	☐	☐	☐
13. How would you rate the quality of the blinds?..	☐	☐	☐	☐	☐	☐
14. How would you rate the quantity of the birds?..	☐	☐	☐	☐	☐	☐
15. How would you rate the overall quality of your field experience?................	☐	☐	☐	☐	☐	☐

	Good	Fair	Poor
16. How would you describe the weather conditions?...	☐	☐	☐

17. Did the Outfitter accurately represent the overall quality of your experience (quality of area, birds, accommodations, etc.)?............................ ☐ Yes ☐ No

18. Did you provide the Outfitter (Guide or Lodge) with truthful statements regarding your personal needs, your skills and your expectations?............... ☐ Yes ☐ No

19. Would you use this Outdoor Professional/Business again?............................ ☐ Yes ☐ No

20. Would you recommend this Outdoor Professional/Business to others?..... ☐ Yes ☐ No

Comments: _____
_____
_____
_____
_____
_____
_____
_____
_____
_____
_____
_____
_____
_____
_____
_____
_____

Will you permit Picked-By-You to use your name and comments in our book(s)? ☐ Yes ☐ No

Signature_____

Index of Guides & Outfitters by Bird Species

Bobwhite

Game Management Services
Longleaf Plantation

Chukar

Catskill Pheasantry
Eagles' Ridge Ranch
Reecer Creek Gamebird Ranch
S + S Hunting Service
Sandhills Adventures
Wapiti River Guides
Warriors Mark Shooting Preserve
Willow Creek Wildlife

Crane, Sandhill

Eagles' Ridge Ranch
Hap's Guide Service
Sandhills Adventures
Western Guiding Service

Dove

Missouri River Ringnecks
Prairie Winds Guide Service
S + S Hunting Service
South Dakota Pheasant Hunts
Willow Creek Wildlife

Duck(s), Mallards and all Dabbling

Big Antler Outfitters
D.C. Outdoor Adventures
Eagle Nest Lodge & Outfitters
Hap's Guide Service
Northern Honker Outfitter
Palmetto Guide Service
Prairie Winds Guide Service
Sandhills Adventures
South Dakota Pheasant Hunts
Sure Shot Guide Service
Western Guiding Service

Goose, Canada

Big Antler Outfitters
D.C. Outdoor Adventures
Eagle Nest Lodge & Outfitters
Eagles' Ridge Ranch
Hap's Guide Service
Northern Honker Outfitter
Prairie Winds Guide Service
S + S Hunting Service
Sandhills Adventures
South Dakota Pheasant Hunts
Sure Shot Guide Service
Willow Creek Wildlife
Western Guiding Service

Goose, Snow

Big Antler Outfitters
Northern Honker Outfitter
Palmetto Guide Service
Sure Shot Guide Service
Western Guiding Service

Index of Guides & Outfitters by Bird Species

Partridge Hungarian (Gray)

Eagle Nest Lodge & Outfitters
Good's Bird Hunts
Sandhills Adventures
South Dakota Pheasant Hunts
Sure Shot Guide Service
Triple B Outfitters
Warriors Mark Shooting Preserve
Western Guiding Service

Prairie Chiken(s)

Missouri River Ringnecks
Prairie Winds Guide Service
S + S Hunting Service
Sandhills Adventures
Willow Creek Wildlife

Sharptail Grouse

Cow Creek Ranch
Eagle Nest Lodge & Outfitters
Good's Bird Hunts
Missouri River Ringnecks
P & R Hunting Lodge
S + S Hunting Service
Sandhills Adventures
Triple B Outfitters
Western Guiding Service
Willow Creek Wildlife

Sage Grouse

Eagle Nest Lodge & Outfitters
Good's Bird Hunts
Triple B Outfitters

Ruffed Grouse

D.C. Outdoor Adventures
Eagles' Ridge Ranch
Libby Sporting Camps
The Hungry Trout
Triple B Outfitters

Pheasant

Catskill Pheasantry
Cow Creek Ranch
D.C. Outdoor Adventures
Don Reeves Pheasant Ranch
Eagle Nest Lodge & Outfitters
Eagles' Ridge Ranch
Good's Bird Hunts
Libby Sporting Camps
Longleaf Plantation
Missouri River Ringnecks
P & R Hunting Lodge
Prairie Winds Guide Service
Reecer Creek Gamebird Ranch
S + S Hunting Service
Sandhills Adventures
South Dakota Pheasant Hunts
Sure Shot Guide Service
Triple B Outfitters
Warriors Mark Shooting Preserve
Willow Creek Wildlife
Western Guiding Service

Index of Guides & Outfitters by Bird Species

Quail, Californian

D.C. Outdoor Adventures
Eagles' Ridge Ranch
Game Management Service
Longleaf Plantation
PrairieWinds Guide Service
Reecer Creek Gamebird Ranch
S + S Hunting Service
Sandhills Adventures
Sure Shot Guide Service
Warriors Mark Shooting Preserve

Quail, Scaled (Blue)

Game Management Services

Snipe

Palmetto Guide Service

Turkey (all sub-species)

Adobe Lodge Hunting Camp
Cow Creek Ranch
D.C. Outdoor Adventures
Echo Canyon Outfitters
Farley's International Adventures
PrairieWinds Guide Service
Sandhills Adventures
S + S Hunting Service
Wild Redheads Archery Turkey
  Hunts

Woodcock

D.C. Outdoor Adventures
Libby Sporting Camps
The Hungry Trout

Duck(s), Sea and Bay

Palmetto Guide Service

Index of Guides & Outfitters by State/Province

Index of Guides & Outfitters by State/Province

Alphabetical Index by Company Name